The Black Arc

THE RINGS OF AKHATEN

By William Shaw

Published April 2020 by Obverse Books

Cover Design © Cody Schell

Text © William Shaw, 2020

Range Editors: Philip Purser-Hallard, Paul Simpson

Recently Published

For everyone who listened patiently.

CONTENTS

OVERVIEW

Serial Title: *The Rings of Akhaten*

Writer: Neil Cross

Director: Farren Blackburn

Original UK Transmission Date: 6 April 2013

Running Time: 43m 45s

UK Viewing Figures: 7.45 million

Regular Cast: Matt Smith (The Doctor), Jenna-Louise Coleman (Clara)

Guest Cast: Michael Dixon (Dave), Nicola Sian (Ellie), Emilia Jones (Merry), Chris Anderson (The Chorister), Aidan Cook (The Mummy), Karl Greenwood (Dor'een)

Antagonists: The Vigil, the Old God

Responses:

'Cross's script is unafraid to tug liberally at the heartstrings; Clara's final saving of the day, sacrificing all her mother's "days that never were" had me choking up, then cheering her on.'

[Dan Martin, *The Guardian*, 6 April 2013]

'With such syrupy gloop sticking underfoot, the story slows so badly that by the 20-minute mark we still haven't got past the head-swaying Muppet choir.'

[Graham Kibble-White, *Doctor Who Magazine*, June 2013]

SYNOPSIS

Curious about his new companion, **the Doctor** covertly observes her parents' courtship and her early life. **Dave** and **Ellie** first meet when a leaf blows into his face and she saves him from being hit by a car. He keeps the leaf and eventually passes it on to their daughter, **Clara**. Years later Clara and Dave stand by Ellie's grave, still watched by the Doctor.

The Doctor returns to collect Clara in the present day, and takes her to the Rings of Akhaten, a string of asteroids orbiting a giant planet. The Rings house, among other things, a marketplace, a huge amphitheatre and a pyramidal Temple, the last a sacred site to a religion that believes life originated on the planet. The market throngs with exotic aliens, who use objects of personal value, backed up by psychometry, as currency. Clara meets **Merry**, a young girl on the run from robed **Choristers** and sinister masked enforcers called the **Vigil**. She tells Clara that she is 'the Queen of Years', chosen to memorise all her people's songs and stories. She is to sing 'the Long Song' at the forthcoming Festival of Offerings, and is terrified of making a mistake and angering 'Grandfather'.

Clara reassures her that she will do well, and persuades her to return to the Choristers. She joins the Doctor for the ceremony in the amphitheatre. The Doctor explains that the Long Song, and the offerings of personal keepsakes given by their fellow celebrants, are supposed to keep an **Old God**, known as 'Grandfather', from awakening. In the Temple, despite the lullaby sung to it by the latest in a never-ending sequence of Choristers, an imprisoned **Mummy** begins to stir. The terrified Merry is caught in a beam of light mid-song, and drawn away through space towards the Temple.

The Doctor and Clara hasten to help. Clara gives up her late mother's ring to rent a spacegoing 'moped' from **Dor'een**, a stallholder. They follow Merry to the Temple, where the Mummy is soon awake and rampaging. They learn that on the occasions when the Old God awakens, the Queen of Years is used as a sacrifice to prevent it from eating everyone else's souls. Despite Merry's protestations, the Doctor and Clara promise to save her. The Vigil arrive to feed the girl to the Old God, but the Doctor holds them off. The Mummy breaks free from its glass case, but instead of attacking it sends a signal to the giant world nearby. The Mummy is merely an alarm system; the Old God is the planet itself, and it is now awake.

Clara returns to the amphitheatre with Merry, who once again begins to sing, while the Doctor faces the living planet. He understands that the legend of the Old God eating 'souls' refers to stories, and challenges it to consume his own. The effort nearly overwhelms it, but then it rallies and grows stronger. Clara returns to offer it her parents' leaf, a symbol of the family's lost future together. The infinite possibilities inherent in this negative offering finally defeat the Old God and it collapses in on itself.

The Doctor returns Clara home, and she confronts him about his presence at her mother's grave. The Doctor produces the ring Clara used to pay Dor'een, and says the people she saved wanted her to have it.

INTRODUCTION

2013 was a landmark year for **Doctor Who**. It saw the programme's 50th anniversary, with many high-profile celebrations and plenty of mainstream press coverage. It saw **Doctor Who** become the UK's most watched TV drama for the year with *The Day of the Doctor*[1]. It saw the return of David Tennant as the 10th Doctor and the revelation of John Hurt as the War Doctor, rewriting **Doctor Who**'s past to an unprecedented degree. It also saw the arrival of Jenna-Louise Coleman as Clara Oswald[2], the longest-serving companion of 21st-century **Doctor Who**, as well as the departure of Matt Smith as the 11th Doctor and the debut of Peter Capaldi as the 12th. All of which raises the question: in the midst of this culturally significant upheaval, why focus on a comparatively minor story like *The Rings of Akhaten*?

This book argues that *The Rings of Akhaten*, dismissed at the time as contrived, sentimental, and 'un-**Doctor Who**'[3], deserves reassessment, and that however flawed their execution, the story's ideas are among the most radical and exciting in the programme's history.

---

[1] '**Doctor Who** 50th Is the Most Watched Drama in 2013'.

[2] This is complicated by Coleman's two prior appearances in *Asylum of the Daleks* (2012) and *The Snowmen* (2012), playing characters who are 'pieces' of the original Clara Oswald. But for our purposes, other than a brief teaser at the end of *The Snowmen*, the character of Clara Oswald made her debut in *The Bells of Saint John* (2013). Meanwhile, as the actor is now known professionally as Jenna Coleman, that name will be used throughout the rest of this book.

[3] Kibble-White, Graham, 'The Rings of Akhaten', *Doctor Who Magazine* (DWM) #460, cover date June 2013, p64.

Specifically, it argues that the episode represents a trenchant (and overdue) engagement with the ideas of New Atheism. Formulated in the late 2000s, but with roots going back to at least the 1970s, New Atheism was spearheaded by thinkers including Richard Dawkins and Sam Harris. Journalist Jacob Hamburger characterises the movement as 'making non-belief and scientific rationality a political cause in the post-9/11 context'[4]. While many of its goals were admirable, the movement was characterised by virulent Islamophobia, among other bigotries. Chapter 1 places *The Rings of Akhaten* in the historical context of New Atheism, and covers the movement's previous relationship with **Doctor Who**. It suggests that the Doctor's rhetoric and behaviour within *The Rings of Akhaten* reflect dominant patterns in New Atheist thought, including the movement's nascent cultural imperialism. Chapter 1 argues that the episode ultimately demonstrates the inadequacy of New Atheism in dealing with the religious oppression it seeks to address.

Chapter 2 moves on to the episode's proffered alternative to New Atheism, namely a kind of feminist solidarity. It explores the episode's conception of Clara Oswald, particularly her definition in terms of storytelling, with a focus on her friendship with Merry Gejelh[5]. It argues that Clara and Merry form a kind of cross-cultural collaboration which is instrumental in defeating the Old God of Akhaten. This relationship echoes the concept of sisterhood as formulated by many feminist theorists, including bell hooks, who

---

[4] Hamburger, Jacob, 'What Was New Atheism?'
[5] Spellings, when not obvious, are taken from *Doctor Who: The Complete History* Volume 73, p19.

argues that 'We can be sisters united by shared interests and beliefs [...] united in our struggle to end sexist oppression, united in political solidarity.'[6]

But the episode's exploration of sisterhood, while a welcome alternative to the flawed worldview of New Atheism, is not without problems of its own. Chapter 3 examines the difficulties with the episode's political vision, and the ways its formulated alternatives reproduce many problems of the systems it critiques. It also examines potential issues with the episode's storytelling choices and its wider cultural context, and the ways they contribute to the episode's reception, both positive and negative.

Finally, Chapter 4 examines *The Rings of Akhaten* in the context of **Doctor Who**'s 50th anniversary. It argues that the episode fits within a larger pattern of anniversary stories which display anxiety about **Doctor Who**'s continued existence. It focuses on Clara as a character, and how the themes and iconography of *The Rings of Akhaten* are repeatedly invoked in Series 7 to solidify the show's ultimate casting-off of this anxiety with a distinctly feminised vision of the future. It also discusses the problems with this feminine futurity in the context of popular media at large, and the ways in which some of this future has already come to pass.

---

[6] hooks, bell, *Feminist Theory: From Margin to Center*, p65.

CHAPTER 1: THE DOCTOR AS NEW ATHEIST

'Hey, do you mind if I tell you a story? One you might not have heard. All the elements in your body were forged many, many millions of years ago, in the heart of a faraway star that exploded and died. That explosion scattered those elements across the desolations of deep space. After so, so many millions of years, these elements came together to form new stars and new planets. And on and on it went. The elements came together, and burst apart, forming shoes, and ships, and sealing wax, and cabbages, and kings! Until eventually, they came together to make you.'

[The Doctor, *The Rings of Akhaten*]

'Think about it. On one planet [...] molecules that would normally make nothing more complicated than a chunk of rock, gather themselves together into chunks of rock-sized matter of such staggering complexity that they are capable [...] of thinking and feeling, and falling in love with yet other chunks of complex matter. We now understand essentially how the trick is done, but only since 1859. [...] Darwin seized the window of the burka and wrenched it open, letting in a flood of understanding whose dazzling novelty, and power to uplift the human spirit, perhaps had no precedent.'

[Richard Dawkins, *The God Delusion* (2006), p411]

Before his turn in *The Stolen Earth* (2008), Richard Dawkins was primarily known for his non-fiction writing. A crucial figure in the so-called New Atheist movement, Dawkins wrote *The God Delusion* two years prior to his appearance on **Doctor Who**. In this book he argues that 'supernatural religion'[7] is untenable in the modern world. He instead advocates for what he calls 'Einsteinian'[8], or, in the above example, Darwinian religion – secular appreciation of the sublime beauty of the universe. That he does so with the analogy of assaulting a woman and forcibly removing her religious dress (referring to human ignorance as the 'Mother of all Burkas'[9]) may help to indicate why New Atheism was, and remains, a controversial movement, and why **Doctor Who** saw fit to tackle it in 2013. But **Doctor Who**'s relationship with New Atheism goes back further than *The Stolen Earth*. Before discussing the critique presented by *The Rings of Akhaten*, it is worth briefly outlining the episode's historical context. Fittingly for a religious movement, we begin at the end of the world.

'A Repeated Meme is Just an Idea'[10]

Early on in *The End of the World* (2005), we hear that Platform One 'forbids the use of weapons, teleportation, and religion'[11]. As well as delivering plot information (the villain Cassandra's scheme hinges on illegal teleportation), this line helps establish the episode's mildly satirical tone. The idea that religion is considered as dangerous as 'weapons' in this future society creates a humorous juxtaposition, a joke at the expense of religion, and implies that this irreverent attitude is the inevitable endpoint of

---

[7] Dawkins, Richard, *The God Delusion*, p34.

[8] Dawkins, *The God Delusion*, p34.

[9] Dawkins, *The God Delusion*, p405.

[10] *The End of the World* (2005).

[11] *The End of the World*.

society's development. This atheistic outlook is endemic to much science fiction, and is associated with one writer in particular: Douglas Adams. Indeed, Platform One itself, where the upper classes gather to watch the Earth being destroyed, strongly evokes Adams' novel *The Restaurant at the End of the Universe* (1980), in which the upper classes gather to watch the universe being destroyed. Russell T Davies acknowledges Adams as an influence on *The End of the World*, albeit an unconscious one: 'some things you love so much, you don't even realise you're using them'. But Davies also draws more explicitly on Dawkins' work:

> 'I was aware of using the word "meme", lifted from the writing of Adams' great friend, Richard Dawkins. I'd like to think that at some point, off-stage, the Doctor explained the concept of a meme to Rose, so that by the end of the series, she's practically creating her own meme, of sorts, with the Bad Wolf.'[12]

Coined by Dawkins in his book *The Selfish Gene* (1976) and returned to in much subsequent work, including *The God Delusion*, memes are a way of understanding the development of human traditions as analogous to how genetics determines the characteristics of a population. Memes are 'units of cultural inheritance'[13], and those that survive do so by a process akin to natural selection, because they are well-adapted to their cultural environment. Religions, therefore, can be understood as collections of memes (or 'memeplexes'[14] analogous to gene complexes in

---

[12] Davies, Russell T, et al, *Doctor Who: The Shooting Scripts*, p49.
[13] Dawkins, *The God Delusion*, p222.
[14] Dawkins, *The God Delusion*, p228.

nature), to which people have devoted themselves. Hence the name of the quasi-religious sect in *The End of the World*: 'the Adherents of the Repeated Meme'. That these Adherents are revealed to be thoughtless robots whom the Doctor dismisses as 'just an idea'[15] indicates the less-than-flattering view of religion shared by Dawkins and Davies.

Davies' use of the meme concept here proved a particularly timely reference. The following year Dawkins presented a documentary series, **The Root of All Evil?** (2006), where he strongly criticised contemporary religion. Later that year, *The God Delusion* was published, with a dedication to Dawkins' late friend, Douglas Adams. Dawkins became a figurehead for a new wave of popular anti-religious sentiment, and 2006 saw this wave christened as the New Atheist movement[16].

'You're Just a Parasite!': Doctor Who and the New Atheist Movement

The New Atheist movement has long and diffuse roots, but most accounts place its beginnings around 2004, with the publication of *The End of Faith* by Sam Harris. This book was subsequently joined by Dawkins' *The God Delusion*, Daniel Dennett's *Breaking the Spell* (2006), and Christopher Hitchens' *God is Not Great* (2007). These were among the movement's most popular mainstream texts, and their authors dubbed themselves the 'Four Horsemen' of New Atheism[17]. Together they spearheaded a renewed popular interest

---

[15] *The End of the World*.

[16] Wolf, Gary, 'The Church of the Non-Believers'.

[17] The four of them met on 30 September 2007 for a roundtable

in atheism and a particular brand of scientific scepticism in the mid-to-late 2000s.

The movement's proponents were politically varied, and tended to overlap with existing secularist and popular scientific movements. American New Atheists, for example, were concerned with preserving the constitutional separation of church and state[18], and the longstanding battle over preventing creationism from being taught in schools[19]. British New Atheists, meanwhile, concerned themselves with problems surrounding faith schools[20], and preventing the NHS from offering homeopathy[21]. It should be noted, given this book's largely critical attitude towards New Atheism, that many of its policy goals were admirable. Secularism is an important feature of civil society, and preventing the spread of misinformation, especially within the education system, is an unambiguous good.

The label 'New Atheism' is itself controversial. The phrase was coined by journalist Gary Wolf in a 2006 article for *Wired*; none of the movement's key figures initially identified as such. In his introduction to the 10th anniversary edition of *The God Delusion*, Dawkins states that 'it isn't clear to me how we differ from old

---

discussion, released on DVD and YouTube as 'The Four Horsemen'. A transcript of the conversation was published in 2019, titled *The Four Horsemen: The Discussion That Sparked an Atheist Revolution*.

[18] Harris, Sam, *The End of Faith: Religion, Terror, and the Future of Reason*, pp153-69.

[19] Dennett, Daniel C, *Breaking the Spell: Religion As a Natural Phenomenon*, p308-9.

[20] Dawkins, *The God Delusion*, pp372-79.

[21] **The Enemies of Reason**: *The Irrational Health Service* (2007).

atheists.'[22] Wolf, for his part, distinguishes them by their more pugilistic attitude to faith:

> 'The New Atheists will not let us ["old atheists"] off the hook simply because we are not doctrinaire believers. They condemn not just belief in God but respect for belief in God. Religion is not only wrong; it's evil.'[23]

Wolf is correct that the movement's chief proponents are openly polemical. Hitchens bombastically asserts that '**religion poisons everything**'[24] (emphasis his), while Dawkins describes the God of the Old Testament as 'arguably the most unpleasant character in all fiction'[25]. Dennett, while markedly less pugnacious, compares religion to the lancet fluke, a parasite found in cattle, arguing that religious people's actions are similarly influenced by 'an idea that has lodged in their brains'[26]. Dennett is also a proponent of Dawkins' meme theory, and the notion of religion as a parasitic idea plays into the Doctor's confrontation with 'Grandfather' in *The Rings of Akhaten*.

For Harris, meanwhile, religion is not just irrational, but an extinction-level threat to the human species. A core argument of *The End of Faith* is that 'technical advances in the art of war [chiefly nuclear proliferation] have finally rendered our religious differences

---

[22] Dawkins, *The God Delusion*, p15.
[23] Wolf, 'The Church of the Non-Believers'.
[24] Hitchens, Christopher, *God is Not Great: How Religion Poisons Everything*, p13.
[25] Dawkins, *The God Delusion*, p51.
[26] Dennett, *Breaking the Spell*, p4.

– and hence our religious **beliefs** – antithetical to our survival'[27] (emphasis his). This starts to get at the broader politics of the New Atheists, which is the most noticeable way in which they differ from 'old atheists'. The New Atheists are consciously writing in a post-9/11 context, and this is where the movement's biggest problems begin to emerge.

The New Atheist movement has been widely accused of Islamophobia, and this claim is supported by the movement's core texts. While presented as critiques of religion in general, many spend a disproportionate amount of time on Islam, and indulge ugly stereotypes of Muslims as particularly violent and irrational. *The End of Faith* begins with a graphic description of a suicide bombing by an anonymous young man, which Harris concludes with this snide note:

> 'These are the facts. This is all we know for certain about the young man. Is there anything else we can infer about him on the basis of his behaviour? Was he popular in school? Was he rich or was he poor? Was he of low or high intelligence? His actions leave no clue at all [...] Why is it so easy, then, so trivially easy – you-could-almost-bet-your-life-on-it easy – to guess the young man's religion?'[28]

The obvious answer being: because you have just blatantly played on your readership's assumed Islamophobia. The book dedicates an entire chapter to 'The Problem with Islam', in which Harris argues that, following 9/11, 'We are at war with Islam'[29]. The book also

---

[27] Harris, *The End of Faith*, pp13-14.
[28] Harris, *The End of Faith*, pp11-12.
[29] Harris, *The End of Faith*, pp108-09.

asserts that 'Life under the Taliban is, to a first approximation, what millions of Muslims around the world want to impose on the rest of us'[30], and endorses the use of torture against suspected terrorists. These views are not taken seriously by terrorism experts[31], and yet here they are, in what is arguably **the** foundational text of the New Atheist movement.

Dawkins and Dennett, while less inclined to explicit calls for war, also indulge Islamophobic tropes, particularly the idea that Islam is uniquely violent among major religions. In *Breaking the Spell*, Dennett argues that while Judaism and Christianity no longer regard death as suitable punishment for apostasy, 'Islam stands alone in its inability to renounce this barbaric doctrine convincingly'[32]. Dawkins, meanwhile, asserts that in the modern world those who disrespect Islam are 'physically threatened, on a scale that no other religion has aspired to since the Middle Ages'[33]. Threats against critics of Islam are, of course, unconscionable, but by invoking 'barbaric doctrine' and 'the Middle Ages,' Dennett and Dawkins play into the xenophobic idea that Islam is somehow incompatible with modernity.

Media scholar Arun Kundnani refers to this as the 'Culturalist' or 'Clash of Civilisations' view of so-called Islamic terrorism, in which:

---

[30] Harris, *The End of Faith*, p203.
[31] Richardson, Louise, *What Terrorists Want: Understanding the Enemy, Containing the Threat*; Kundnani, Arun, *The Muslims Are Coming!: Islamophobia, Extremism and the Domestic War on Terror*.
[32] Dennett, *Breaking the Spell*, p289. This claim rests on dubious theological evidence.
[33] Dawkins, *The God Delusion*, p49.

'Muslim politics can be explained simply as the mechanical and repetitive expression of an underlying cultural abstraction called Islam that is preprogrammed for fanaticism, has remained the same over centuries, and whose content can be known through a reading of its religious texts.'[34]

Such views are not only heavily racialised, but also, Kundnani argues, counterproductive in combating terrorism, promoting an inaccurate view of real-world politics and implying that progress is impossible. This ties into a wider criticism of the New Atheists: that their totalising view of rationality facilitates too-easy dismissal of their opposition. Steven Poole identifies this in Harris' rejection of the idea of a religious scientist[35], while Dan Hind identifies the New Atheist worldview with a vulgarised and historically inaccurate view of the Enlightenment:

'The structure of the Folk Enlightenment, in which the rational faces the irrational across a great divide, all too easily serves to discredit legitimate criticism by conflating it with irrationalism.'[36]

Hitchens, for his part, was given to more overtly racist scaremongering. In 2007 he wrote an article for *Vanity Fair* entitled 'Londonistan Calling'. In this piece he asserts that the increased presence of 'Algerians, Bangladeshis, and others' in the Finsbury

---

[34] Kundnani, *The Muslims are Coming!*, p57.
[35] Poole, Steven, '*The Four Horsemen* Review – Whatever Happened to "New Atheism"?'
[36] Hind, Dan, *The Threat to Reason: How the Enlightenment was Hijacked and How We Can Reclaim It*, p155.

Park area of London has made it 'another country,' and that these immigrants bring 'a religion which is not ashamed to speak of conquest and violence'[37]. Kundnani calls this 'an apparent warning... of what happens when Islam is accorded too much tolerance'[38]. Hitchens dismisses the term 'Islamophobia' as 'meaningless' in the same article, but his depiction of immigrants 'Islamising' a European city (not to mention his conflation of Islamic extremism with Muslims per se) is difficult to read as anything else[39]. *God is Not Great* makes similarly dubious and racially-charged claims, including an attempt to argue that 'In no real [...] sense'[40] was the Rev Dr Martin Luther King Jr a Christian.

All of this is important to bear in mind: New Atheism, from the very beginning, contained a deeply reactionary streak, which manifested in racism and Islamophobia. It uncritically parroted an assertion which has been present in European culture since at least the early 19th century, and which postcolonial theorist Edward Said identified in his book *Orientalism* (1978): 'the theme of Europe teaching the Orient the meaning of liberty'[41]. Harris openly makes a version of this claim: 'It is time for us to admit that not all cultures are at the same stage of moral development'[42]. In Harris' view, given the lesser moral development of Islamic cultures, Western powers are justified in using military force (even a nuclear 'first

[37] Hitchens, Christopher, 'Londonistan Calling'.

[38] Kundnani, *The Muslims are Coming!*, p9.

[39] Hitchens, 'Londonistan Calling'.

[40] Hitchens, *God is Not Great*, p176.

[41] Said, Edward W, *Orientalism*, p172.

[42] Harris, *The End of Faith*, p143.

strike'[43]) against them. Hitchens was similarly explicit in his support for the 2003 invasion of Iraq, arguing that the US was justified in taking military action against 'fascism with an Islamic face'[44]. According to the New Atheists, Muslims are inherently prone to violence and tyranny, due to the very nature of their religion, and it is the duty of enlightened Western liberals to show them the error of their ways, by force if necessary. Again, these ideas are not new – hence Edward Said identifying similar strains in Western politics decades earlier. Nonetheless, they experienced a surge in popularity roughly coincident with the revival of **Doctor Who** under Russell T Davies, and Dawkins in particular was a clear source of inspiration.

'We've Travelled'[45]: The Rise and Fall of Dawkinsian Doctor Who

Dawkins' influence over Davies' **Doctor Who** is by no means limited to *The End of the World*. As previously mentioned, the meme concept was an explicit model for the 'Bad Wolf' phrase which helps structure the first 21st-century series. Davies' use of the meme necessarily deviates from its original formulation; Dawkins cuts against the idea of specific 'meme authors,' like Rose in *Bad Wolf / The Parting of the Ways* (2005). But the use of Dawkins' ideas in **Doctor Who** is indicative of a general upsurge in Dawkins' cultural cachet around this time. As the New Atheist movement continued to grow in popularity, 'Torchwood', 'Mr Saxon', and the legends of disappearing planets became the 'memes' of Series 2, 3,

---

[43] Harris, *The End of Faith*, p129.
[44] Hitchens, Christopher, 'Defending Islamofascism'.
[45] *The Stolen Earth*.

and 4 respectively. Media scholar Dee Amy-Chinn argues that Davies' version of the meme functions as 'the repeated cultural trope on which new **Who** is built'[46]. Dawkins' work was not just window dressing: it was integral to the structure of **Doctor Who** in this period.

The New Atheist influence is also visible in some of Davies' individual **Doctor Who** episodes. *Bad Wolf / The Parting of the Ways* introduces an army of Daleks who have explicitly embraced the trappings of religion. They command Rose, 'Do not blaspheme,' and demand 'worship' of their Dalek Emperor, who claims to be 'the God of all Daleks!' This is a take on the Daleks unlike any in 20th-century **Doctor Who** (the Doctor even asks, 'Since when did the Daleks have a concept of blasphemy?'[47]), and can be read as an outgrowth of contemporary fears of religious extremism. These same fears underpin much New Atheist rhetoric, and even if there is no direct influence, both speak to the same culture at roughly the same time.

Gridlock (2007) deals more directly with real-world religion, including the Christian hymns 'The Old Rugged Cross' and 'Abide With Me' at key points in the narrative. One might expect, given the dismissive views of religion held by both Davies and the New Atheists, that these songs would be treated as a sham, an opiate to the deceived masses of New Earth. But in talking about the episode

---

[46] Amy-Chinn, Dee, 'Davies, Dawkins, and Deus Ex TARDIS: Who Finds God in the Doctor?', in Hansen, Christopher J, ed, *Ruminations, Peregrinations and Regenerations: A Critical Approach to Doctor Who*, p31.
[47] *Bad Wolf / The Parting of the Ways.*

with podcaster Toby Hadoke, Davies states his willingness to avoid this interpretation: 'You mustn't do that sixth form writing... the satirical version where they all sing "The Old Rugged Cross", and the Doctor does a speech about how "You're all enslaved by your religion!"'[48]

This willingness to use 'The Old Rugged Cross' so straightforwardly may seem counter-intuitive, but it accords with many New Atheists who are vocal in their appreciation of religious art. Dawkins, for example, relays this anecdote in *The God Delusion*:

> 'I was once the guest of the week on a British radio show called **Desert Island Discs**. You have to choose the eight records you would take with you if marooned on a desert island. Among my choices was "Mache dich mein Herze rein" from Bach's *St Matthew Passion* [1727]. The interviewer was unable to understand how I could choose religious music without being religious. You might as well say, how can you enjoy *Wuthering Heights* [1847] when you know perfectly well that Cathy and Heathcliff never really existed?'[49]

Davies states that he used 'The Old Rugged Cross' in *Gridlock* because:

> 'I think I'd been to a funeral, and I'd heard it, and I thought, "What a beautiful song." [...] No wonder hymns work, because they're absolutely beautiful. [...] I think it's a shame that only the religious get those songs. I think it's a shame

---

[48] Quoted in Hadoke, Toby, 'Russell T Davies: Part 5'. **Toby Hadoke's Who's Round** #124.
[49] Dawkins, *The God Delusion*, p111.

that you have to be a Christian to enjoy "The Old Rugged Cross", because it's beautiful, and the sense of community it suggests and engenders is lovely. And why do you get that and atheists don't have it? I'll have a bit of that, thank you very much.'[50]

This attitude is clearly similar to, if not influenced by, Dawkins' pronouncement that 'If there is a logical argument linking the existence of great art to the existence of God, it is not spelled out by its proponents'[51]. The New Atheists are not averse to religious art – they simply reject the faith which underpins it.

The most visible incursion of Dawkins into Davies' **Doctor Who** is, of course, his aforementioned cameo in *The Stolen Earth*. Here Dawkins plays himself as a talking head on the fictional television programme *Universally Speaking*: 'But it's an empirical fact. The planets didn't come to us, we came to them. Just look at the stars. We're in a completely different region of space. We've travelled.'[52] This cameo, part of a montage of televisual responses to the Earth being stolen, is indicative of Dawkins' contemporary position in popular culture. Not only is he a familiar face on UK television (comparable with Paul O'Grady, who succeeds him in the montage), he is used here as a kind of shorthand for scientific rationality, demonstrating that the crisis is taken seriously by the planet's best and brightest. This cameo marks the peak of Dawkins' significance for **Doctor Who**, coinciding with the popular peak of New Atheism.

While the New Atheist movement continued to be active, and its

---

[50] Quoted in Hadoke, Toby, 'Russell T Davies: Part 5'.
[51] Dawkins, *The God Delusion*, p111.
[52] *The Stolen Earth*.

Four Horsemen continued to publish, New Atheism's popular relevance significantly diminished from around 2008 onwards. The end of the evangelical-influenced Bush presidency removed one of the movement's biggest targets, and the ongoing fallout from the 2008 financial crisis pushed its concerns down the news agenda. On top of this, shifts in public opinion on the Iraq War took some of the shine off Hitchens' and Harris' foreign policy analysis, and Hitchens' death in 2011 meant the movement lost one of its most high-profile advocates. The result was a decline in New Atheism's relevance, and we can see this paralleled in its shrinking influence over **Doctor Who**.

Steven Moffat took over as Executive Producer of **Doctor Who** from *The Eleventh Hour* (2010), and in the subsequent years he moved the programme away from the meme-inspired 'arc phrases' Davies had introduced. His one explicit reference to Dawkins comes in his first series finale, *The Big Bang* (2010), and is somewhat less reverent than Davies' treatment. In an alternate universe where stars do not exist, the young Amelia Pond is viewed as eccentric for believing in them. She overhears some concerned adults:

CHRISTINE

It's quite common, actually. Throughout history, people have talked about seeing stars in the sky. God knows where it comes from.

SHARON

I just don't want her growing up and joining one of those

Star Cults. I don't trust that Richard Dawkins.[53]

This gag, like the *Stolen Earth* cameo, relies on Dawkins' reputation for scientific rationalism. The joke is an indication of the strangeness of this alternate universe: here Dawkins is seen as an anti-science crank, rather than the arch-sceptic he is in our world. However, since both the young Amelia Pond and the viewer know that there ought to be stars in the sky, Dawkins remains in the right[54]. Still, the diminishment of Dawkins from a bona fide cameo to a joking reference marks an early point in the long-term downward slump the New Atheist movement had begun by the early 2010s.

As New Atheism's popular relevance waned, its reactionary tendencies became more pronounced. This has recently prompted several former New Atheists to publicly sever ties with the movement. In 2017 scientist Phil Torres expressed his disillusionment with the New Atheists:

> 'They say they care about facts, yet refuse to change their beliefs when inconvenient data are presented [...] And they apparently don't give a damn about alienating women and people of color, a truly huge demographic of potential allies in the battle against religious absurdity.'[55]

Popular scientist and former New Atheist blogger PZ Myers also disavowed the movement in 2019. He criticised New Atheism's

---

[53] *The Big Bang*.

[54] The notion of star sightings as a recurring phenomenon 'throughout history' also chimes with Dawkins' meme theory.

[55] Torres, Phil, 'From the Enlightenment to the Dark Ages: How "New Atheism" Slid Into the Alt-Right'.

'active neglect of social justice issues' such as feminism, and argued that the movement had become 'a shambles of alt-right memes and dishonest hucksters mangling science to promote racism, sexism, and bloody regressive politics'[56].

Myers was responding to an article called 'What Was New Atheism?'[57]. As this title suggests, the New Atheist movement is now effectively over. While Dawkins, Dennett, and Harris continue working, and many former New Atheists still campaign on the same political issues, the singular cultural moment of New Atheism has passed. The prevalence of casual bigotry, and even allegations of sexual assault[58], drove many away from the movement, and several former members have either left the movement, or drifted into other, more reactionary ones. (Harris, for example, has become a figurehead for the so-called 'Intellectual Dark Web'[59], a set of loosely-aligned media reactionaries).

All of this meant that, by 2013, the New Atheist movement had largely faded from prominence, but was a recent enough memory to allow critical engagement with the benefit of hindsight. **Doctor Who**, a programme which initially embraced New Atheism only to move away from it, would prove the ideal venue in which to do this.

---

[56] Myers, PZ, 'The Train Wreck That Was the New Atheism'.
[57] Hamburger, 'What Was New Atheism?'
[58] Oppenheimer, Mark, 'Will Misogyny Bring Down The Atheist Movement?'
[59] Weiss, Bari, 'Meet the Renegades of the Intellectual Dark Web'.

'On That Planet': *The Rings of Akhaten* and the Politics of Setting

As we have seen, the Doctor's rhetoric throughout *The Rings of Akhaten* owes much to New Atheism. His emphasis on the wonders of the natural universe, as opposed to religious wonder, mirrors Dawkins' belief in 'Einsteinian religion,' and his angry reference to the Old God as 'just a parasite' echoes Daniel Dennett's comparison of religion to a 'little brain worm'[60]. But before we examine the implications of these New Atheist talking points, it is worth noting how appropriate Matt Smith's Doctor is for this story.

Semiotically, the 11th Doctor is manifestly an establishment figure. He is not only a white man, but a tweedy, bookish type in a bow tie and leather elbow patches. Jon Arnold connects him with the 'young fogey,' a term referring to 'relatively young and generally conservative men who dress and often act in old fashioned ways'[61]. Both fandom and the press tend to describe Smith's Doctor with joking reference to academia. Tom Phillips at the *New Statesman* calls him 'a dotty professor'[62], while Fraser McAlpine at BBC America describes him as an 'eccentric child-like professor'[63]. An early version of this description appears in Moffat's account of Smith's audition for the part: 'boffin and action hero, schoolboy and

---

[60] Dennett, *Breaking the Spell*, p3.

[61] Arnold, Jon, *The Black Archive #19: The Eleventh Hour*, p25.

[62] Phillips, Tom, 'Matt Smith: the Rise and Fall of the Hipster Doctor'.

[63] McAlpine, Fraser, 'The Secret of Matt Smith's Success as the 11th Doctor'.

professor, hot young guy and ancient wizard.'[64] Smith's Doctor is a youthful version of the image presented by Richard Dawkins the distinguished Oxford don, or Christopher Hitchens the self-conscious public intellectual.

More broadly, the 11th Doctor's status as a brilliant upper-class white man who goes around 'fixing' other cultures has some obvious resonances with the New Atheist worldview, and is generally queasy in a postcolonial context, given its resemblance to how British colonialists tended to view themselves. To be fair, this description applies to most, if not all, versions of the Doctor to date. Media scholar John Vohlidka describes the Doctor as 'a champion of Western ideals', who uses 'his superior Western scientific knowledge to liberate the inferior natives'[65]. But the 11th Doctor has particularly strong ties to the same quaint Englishness channelled by the New Atheists.

With this in mind, it is worth examining the culture of Akhaten before we assess how the Doctor interacts with it. Discussing *The Rings of Akhaten* with journalist Benjamin Cook, Neil Cross emphasises the episode's setting:

> 'They wanted the episode – which is Clara's first alien adventure, really – to be as big, and grand, and running-around-y, and alien as possible. A really, properly alien planet, which was a massive challenge. A lot of fun. Once I had a sense of the planet – and the rings, and the church [...]

---

[64] Moffat, Steven, 'Production Notes', DWM #405, cover date March 2009, p11.
[65] Vohlidka, John, '**Doctor Who** and the Critique of Western Imperialism', in Orthia, Lindy, ed, *Doctor Who and Race*, p126.

– I began to construct a story around it.'[66]

There is an interesting tension in this statement. Cross simultaneously stresses the importance of worldbuilding, and leaves the content of that worldbuilding loosely defined. He refers to Akhaten primarily through archetypal nouns: 'the planet,' 'the rings,' 'the church' (although there is some ambiguity as to whether 'the church' refers to the Pyramid itself or the institution of the Choristers). Some of this vagueness can be attributed to the interview's status as a promotional teaser, but that sense of the nebulously, 'properly alien' informs the production at large, to the point where one draft of the script was named simply 'Alien Planet'[67].

This may indicate that Cross' focus on worldbuilding was misguided. The Davies and Moffat eras' 45-minute single-episode stories do not lend themselves to lengthy explorations of their settings. Moreover, exploration has not been the dominant mode of **Doctor Who** since the Hartnell era. Lacking the lengthy combined runtime of stories like *The Web Planet* or *The Space Museum* (both 1965), there are moments of *The Rings of Akhaten* that betray a less-than-elegant fusion of setting and story. The 'Nimmer's Door' out of the Pyramid, for example, is introduced, associated with an Akhaten folk tale, and sung open by Merry over the course of three lines. Nevertheless, the decision to foreground the setting, and therefore to de-emphasise the Doctor, has real political significance, given his position as a Western intellectual outsider.

---

[66] Quoted in Cook, Benjamin, 'The Rings of Akhaten'. DWM #459, cover date May 2013, p14.

[67] *The Complete History* Volume 73, p15.

Cross' ostensible focus on the totally alien also belies the degree to which Akhaten draws on existing cultures, especially Middle Eastern ones. The most obvious inspiration is Ancient Egypt. Kate Orman observes that the very name 'Akhaten' is 'a play on the name of the pharaoh Akhenaten, and surely Merry, the Queen of Years, takes her name from his daughter, Meritaten'[68]. Pharaoh Akhenaten, also known as Amenhotep IV, is an important figure in Ancient Egyptian history. Ruling Egypt for 17 years in the 14th century BCE[69], he is notable for, among other things, introducing a new quasi-monotheistic religion called Atenism, based around a god called the Aten, or 'the living sun-disc,' whose name was often preceded in royal inscriptions with 'my father lives'. Historian Jacobus van Dijk notes that Akhenaten introduced:

> 'a radically new way of depicting a god – as a disc with rays ending in hands that touch the king and his family, extending symbols of life and power towards them and receiving their offerings.'[70]

The visual similarities to the Old God of Akhaten, which is also a glowing disc that emits rays to receive offerings, is striking, as is the shared emphasis on patriarchal lineage. Akhaten's Old God is also known as Grandfather, echoing the Aten's association with

---

[68] Orman, Kate, *The Black Archive #12: Pyramids of Mars*, p62.

[69] Precise dates are difficult to ascertain, but historians generally place his reign at either 1353–36 or 1351–34 BCE.

[70] Van Dijk, Jacobus, 'The Amarna Period and the Later New Kingdom' (c 1352-1069 BC), in Shaw, Ian, ed, *The Oxford History of Ancient Egypt*, pp267-68.

Akhenaten's father, Amenhotep III[71].

Akhenaten's reign also saw the emergence of a new and distinctive type of art, known as the Amarna style, after the city and holy site Akhenaten established for his new quasi-monotheistic state religion. This style was characterised by spindly human figures with exaggerated extremities, and Van Dijk notes that depictions of the royal family in this period 'display an intimacy such as had never before been shown in Egyptian art [...] They kiss and embrace under the beneficent rays of the Aten, whose love pervades all of his creation'[72]. The Amarna style has been widely appropriated by Western science fiction and fantasy media, where tall, thin humanoid figures with exaggerated heads and hands often serve as visual shorthand for alien art or civilisations, as do images of figures gathered around suns or other celestial bodies. One particularly blatant example is the **Battlestar Galactica** story *Lost Planet of the Gods* (1978). The story features an ancient planet named Kobol, said to be the 'mother world of all humans', whose abandoned Egyptian-style pyramids are marked with the seal of 'the Ninth Lord of Kobol,'[73] which is clearly modelled on the Aten.

But Akhaten is more than simply Ancient Egypt in space; the episode draws on a broad array of Eastern cultures and mythologies. The Tiaanamaat market, for example, which the Doctor and Clara explore early on, owes a clear visual debt to depictions of Turkish bazaars or Moroccan markets in Western

---

[71] Akhenaten's queen, Nefertiti, appears earlier in Series 7 in *Dinosaurs on a Spaceship* (2012).

[72] Van Dijk, 'The Amarna Period and the Later New Kingdom', p274.

[73] **Battlestar Galactica**: *Lost Planet of the Gods* episode 2.

adventure fiction. The name 'Tiaanamaat' evokes the ancient Babylonian goddess Tiamat; the Doctor even identifies some 'Pan-Babylonians' among the market browsers[74]. Additionally, the name echoes both the Ancient Egyptian goddess Ma'at, against whose feather the souls of the dead are weighed in the afterlife, and the Mandarin Chinese word 'tiān', meaning heaven. Even the Pyramid of the Rings of Akhaten, the most blatantly 'Egyptian' aspect of the setting, is described in the shooting script as 'More Mesoamerican than Egyptian'[75]. Farren Blackburn's Director's Statement says of the setting, 'maybe it's Aztec, possibly Inca or Ancient Egyptian, who knows for sure'[76], further blending the Americas with the 'Eastern' milieu of the rest of the episode. The mummy-like creature inside the Pyramid, meanwhile, clearly invokes depictions of Egypt in Western pulp fiction[77], while the domes and flat roofs visible behind the amphitheatre invoke a vaguely 'Middle Eastern' architecture.

Historian Matthew Kilburn argues that The Vampires of Venice (2010) 'dines à la carte on history; its relation to the Venice of 1580 is supportive to its manipulation of 20th-century genre conventions.'[78] Here we see a similar dynamic, but with even less

---

[74] Along with a 'Lugal-Irra-Kush', whose name echoes the ancient Nubian Kingdom of Kush.

[75] The Complete History Volume 73, p17.

[76] See Appendix 3.

[77] As well as the mummies of the Inca civilisation and several others from around the world.

[78] Kilburn, Matthew, 'Genealogies across Time: History and Storytelling in Steven Moffat's Doctor Who', in O'Day, Andrew, ed, Doctor Who: The Eleventh Hour – A Critical Celebration of the Matt Smith and Steven Moffat Era, p60.

historic or geographical specificity; a scramble of real and imagined versions of multiple cultures across different regions and time periods. Combined, these disparate elements create a timeless, abstracted, fictionalised version of 'the East'. Or, more precisely, of 'the Orient'.

This brings us back to Edward Said. In *Orientalism*, Said argues that Western writing about 'the East' has historically tended to reinforce an intellectual paradigm, or discourse, wherein these regions are understood not in terms of their own history and culture, but in terms of the West's relationship to them. He calls this discourse Orientalism, and argues that it historically arises from power differentials between the two regions. These power relations are expressed in the overriding tropes of Orientalism:

> 'The Oriental is irrational, depraved (fallen), childlike, "different"; thus the European is rational, virtuous, mature, "normal." But the way of enlivening the relationship was everywhere to stress the fact that the Oriental lived in a different but thoroughly organized world of his own, a world with its own national, cultural, and epistemological boundaries and principles of internal coherence. Yet what gave the Oriental's world its intelligibility and identity was not the result of his own efforts but rather the whole complex series of knowledgeable manipulations by which the Orient was identified by the West. [...] Knowledge of the Orient, because generated out of strength, in a sense **creates** the Orient, the Oriental, and his world'[79].

---

[79] Said, *Orientalism*, p40.

Said argues that 'the Orient studied was a textual universe by and large'[80], responding 'more to the culture that produced it [i.e. the West] than to its putative object'[81]. Orientalist fiction represents an extension of this scholarly principle. It treats these regions and their histories as 'a theatrical stage affixed to Europe'[82], a set of iconography which provides a spectacular backdrop for European stories, rather than stories meaningfully about the 'Orient' itself.

We see this dynamic at work in *The Rings of Akhaten*, which creates a world with clear reference to Eastern histories and mythologies, but draws more heavily on Western adventure fiction than on those Eastern mythologies themselves. The planet's profusion of colourful aliens earned this episode many comparisons to *Star Wars* (1977), which production designer Michael Pickwoad acknowledges as an influence, as well as the 'space films of the 60s and 70s'[83] generally. Prosthetics designer Neill Gorton compares the Tiaanamaat market to 'the *Star Wars* cantina'[84], while Farren Blackburn describes the episode as 'Indiana Jones in space... *Raiders* [*of the Lost Ark*] meets *The Mummy* versus *Prometheus* with a hint of *Blade Runner* for good measure.'[85] The iconic posters for the **Indiana Jones** films clearly inspired the episode's own pseudo-movie poster[86], and the Doctor grabbing his sonic screwdriver as the Pyramid's door closes

---

[80] Said, *Orientalism*, p52.

[81] Said, *Orientalism*, p22.

[82] Said, *Orientalism*, p63.

[83] Hadoke, Toby, 'Michael Pickwoad'. **Toby Hadoke's Who's Round #138.**

[84] *The Complete History* Volume 73, p21.

[85] See Appendix 3.

[86] 'Epic Images for the New Adventures'.

behind him references similar moments in a number of **Indiana Jones** films.

As well as these American franchises, *The Rings of Akhaten* echoes the early years of **Doctor Who**. The Doctor explicitly references Susan early in the episode, while the Mesoamerican-inspired design elements and the plot's turning on sacrifice recall *The Aztecs* (1964). *The Keys of Marinus* (1964) also looms curiously large, both with the prominence of 'psychometry' (a word that first appears in **Doctor Who** during that serial), and the fact that *The Rings of Akhaten* opens its depiction of an alien world with an impressive pyramid[87].

Star Wars, **Indiana Jones** and **Doctor Who** are themselves heirs to the Orientalist traditions identified by Said, borrowing heavily from depictions of Egypt and other Middle Eastern regions in 19th- and early 20th-century pulp fiction as well as 20th-century film serials. Postcolonial theorist Robert JC Young describes Orientalism as 'a representation of another culture without reference to the original'[88]. In referencing popular American films and old **Doctor Who** just as, if not more, explicitly than actual Egyptian culture, *The Rings of Akhaten* places itself in this same tradition.

All of which is to say that there is something profoundly uncomfortable about the idea that, in seeking to depict a 'properly

---

[87] On top of this, *The Rings of Akhaten*'s status as a (primarily) studio-bound story about exploring an unfamiliar planet is arguably closer to a Hartnell-era production model than most of the 21st-century series.

[88] Young, Robert JC, *Postcolonialism: A Very Short Introduction*, p141.

alien' place, **Doctor Who** should opt for a Westernised version of 'the East'. This replicates the same intellectual and political dynamics Said identifies in *Orientalism*, which are repeated, mostly uncritically, by New Atheism. In doing so, however, *The Rings of Akhaten* explicitly calls attention to the Doctor's attitude towards Akhaten's culture, and so can be read as commenting on these Orientalist traditions even as it invokes them.

It is telling that the Doctor presents Akhaten first and foremost as a spectacle. He chooses it as a destination when Clara requests 'something awesome,'[89] and he ostentatiously counts down to the 'reveal' of the Pyramid. The episode in general is heavy on visual splendour, with its profusion of exotic aliens and sweeping CGI vistas, which the Doctor excitedly describes.

This was a significant line in many critiques of the episode. In his review for *Doctor Who Magazine*, Graham Kibble-White argues that the story 'takes a specifically un-**Doctor Who** approach to its creations, turning the aliens into a freak show, something to be goggled at, rather than truly met'[90]. This correctly identifies the episode's focus, but hits a rather troubling snag: what, precisely, is 'un-**Doctor Who**' about the idea of freakish aliens? From *The Daleks* (1963-64) onwards, **Doctor Who** has incorporated the spectacularly alien (or 'bug-eyed monsters'[91] in Sydney Newman's fabled terminology), as a core part of its narratives. The spectacular vistas and grunting, growling, bleeping aliens of Akhaten are firmly in the

---

[89] All quotes from *The Rings of Akhaten* unless otherwise noted.
[90] Kibble-White, '*The Rings of Akhaten*', p64.
[91] Newman, Sydney, quoted in Sullivan, Shannon Patrick, '*The Daleks*'.

tradition of stories like *The Web Planet* or *The End of the World*. The argument that Akhaten's inhabitants are not 'truly met' ignores that this same dynamic underpins some of **Doctor Who**'s most iconic stories. In its presentation of an alien spectacle, *The Rings of Akhaten* draws on an imperialist dynamic that is common within **Doctor Who**: the Doctor's ability to swan into a culture he knows next to nothing about, and casually take control. And, indeed, for the audience to goggle at the spectacle as he does it.

But the episode subverts these assumptions in key ways, which tie back to Cross' insistence on building his world first and introducing the Doctor and Clara second. Said writes of Orientalist discourse that, for the occupier, 'knowledge gives power, more power requires more knowledge, and so on in an increasingly profitable dialectic of information and control'[92]. Yet the Doctor's knowledge of Akhaten is remarkably incomplete, denying him power over the situation (even though we are explicitly told he has been here before). We are used to seeing the Doctor casually rattle off facts about alien civilisations, so to see him reading his history off the back of an envelope – as he does during the Festival of Offerings – feels subtly wrong, as does his half-hearted, badly-timed attempt to join in with the Long Song. He is able to recognise individual alien species, including 'a Hooloovoo,' in a nod to Douglas Adams' *The Hitchhiker's Guide to the Galaxy* (1979), but he refers to the fruit at the market as 'exotic fruit of some description,' betraying his imperfect local knowledge.

Even Dor'een, whose barks and growls are seemingly immune to TARDIS translation, helps reinforce the degree to which the Doctor

---

[92] Said, *Orientalism*, p36.

and Clara are outsiders on Akhaten. It is also notable that while the Doctor is able to communicate with Dor'een, and identifies the local currency as working via 'psychometry,' he is unable or unwilling to trade with her because he lacks any objects of sentimental value, bar the sonic screwdriver[93]. He can observe and interact, but he cannot participate.

By invoking the Orientalist spectacle, but denying its usual ease of comprehension, having it be something the Doctor and Clara (and the viewer) must actively work to understand, *The Rings of Akhaten* highlights the troubling implications of **Doctor Who**'s usual treatment of 'alien' cultures. Kate Orman speculates on the comparative lack of Egyptian-set stories in **Doctor Who**, arguing that one explanation may be the intellectual challenge involved. 'A visit to Egypt, even a simulated one, would not only be costly, it would make the companion (and the viewer) an outsider, obliged to try to understand and fit into an "alien" world'[94]. This is precisely the dynamic at play in *The Rings of Akhaten*, albeit with a more literally alien setting. It is not that the aliens of Akhaten can't be met, but that we need to learn to meet them halfway.

'It's a Nice Story': The New Atheist Doctor and the Nature of Belief

The Doctor displays a more specifically New Atheist attitude in his

---

[93] Although he arguably has another item to exchange: Amy's glasses, which are not referenced in these scenes, but which the Doctor wears elsewhere in the episode. His failure to consider giving them up may be simple forgetfulness, or an active refusal to trade away a memento of Amy.

[94] Orman, *Pyramids of Mars*, p35.

patronising approach to the religion of Akhaten[95]. In an early scene, he recounts one of the religion's core beliefs, 'that life in the universe originated here, on that planet.' When Clara asks if this is true, he replies, 'It's what they believe. It's a nice story.' This kind of dismissal is common in New Atheist discourse – Sam Harris asserts that conflicts between India and Pakistan occur because 'they disagree about "facts" that are every bit as fanciful as the names of Santa's reindeer'[96] – and, coming from the Doctor, it is troubling for a number of reasons.

Firstly, it misunderstands the nature of religion. Literary theorist Terry Eagleton criticises the New Atheists for holding what he calls 'the Yeti view of belief in God'. That is, they understand religion only as a belief in the concrete truth of a specific body, the way one might believe in the Yeti, or the Loch Ness Monster. Since the evidence for God's concrete existence is about as strong as the evidence for the Yeti, religious people, in this view, 'have to put up with something less than certainty, known as faith.'[97] Eagleton identifies this tendency in Daniel Dennett, who defines religions as **'social systems whose participants avow belief in a supernatural agent or agents whose approval is to be sought'**[98] (emphasis his). Eagleton comments that this is 'rather like beginning a history of

---

[95] The Doctor refers to the Pyramid as a holy site for 'the Sun Singers of Akhet', but there is ambiguity as to whether this name refers to the religion generally, or the institution of the choristers.
[96] Harris, *The End of Faith*, p26-7.
[97] Eagleton, Terry, *Reason, Faith, and Revolution: Reflections on the God Debate*, p110-11.
[98] Dennett, *Breaking the Spell*, p9.

the potato by defining it as a rare species of rattlesnake'[99]. Instead, Eagleton argues that 'religious faith is not in the first place a matter of subscribing to the proposition that a Supreme Being exists', and that:

> 'faith is for the most part performative rather than propositional. Christians certainly believe that there is a God. But this is not what the credal statement "I believe in God" means. It resembles an utterance like "I have faith in you" more than it does a statement like "I have a steadfast conviction that some goblins are gay."'[100]

While Eagleton's phrasing is somewhat crass, we can at least concede that religious belief tends to be more complex than the New Atheist definition allows, and is influenced by a number of historical and socioeconomic factors that the 'Yeti view' ignores. It is thus odd to see the Doctor dismissing the Akhaten religion so casually, given his own extensive experience with disparate histories[101].

Secondly, this view further contributes to already-ingrained racism. The view of other cultures as backwards and childlike, in need of care and protection by advanced, mature Westerners is prevalent in the Enlightenment tradition to which New Atheism frequently lays claim. Liberal intellectual John Stuart Mill's influential essay *On Liberty* (1859), for example, contains this troubling passage:

---

[99] Eagleton, *Reason, Faith and Revolution*, p50.
[100] Eagleton, *Reason, Faith and Revolution*, p111.
[101] To say nothing of the fact he has actually met both the Yeti and the Loch Ness Monster.

'It is, perhaps, hardly necessary to say that this doctrine [Civil Liberty] is meant to apply only to human beings in the maturity of their faculties. We are not speaking of children, or of young persons below the age which the law may fix as that of manhood or womanhood. Those who are still in a state to require being taken care of by others, must be protected against their own actions as well as against external injury. For the same reason, we may leave out of consideration those backward states of society in which the race itself may be considered as in its nonage.'[102]

Mill advocates civil liberty, but only for those he deems sufficiently advanced to handle it responsibly; a category which explicitly excludes colonised peoples. This is a deeply ugly aspect of Liberalism, designed to justify colonialism, and it's one that New Atheism, mostly uncritically, repeats. This is what Sam Harris refers to when he invokes different levels of moral development to justify military action against 'less mature' societies. The view of a culture or race as simultaneously exotically ancient and childishly incapable may at first seem contradictory, but Said posits it as a core feature of Orientalism. For the Orientalist, the Orient is both 'older and younger than we Europeans.'[103] This gives double justification for European colonisers, making them simultaneously preservers of ancient 'Oriental' civilisations and benevolent guardians of contemporary 'Oriental' peoples. For the Doctor to uncritically repeat this outlook makes his view of Akhaten seem suspect from

---

[102] Mill, John Stuart, *On Liberty, Utilitarianism, and Other Essays*, p13.
[103] Said, *Orientalism*, p168.

the get-go, even if he is not as blatant as Mill in diagnosing the immaturity of the locals.

But the Doctor's comment is perhaps most troubling in the context of **Doctor Who** itself, particularly the Moffat era. Moffat has repeatedly defined the show in terms of children's literature and fairy tale, remarking that '**Doctor Who** doesn't take place in outer space or the future, it takes place under your bed'[104]. The Doctor's dismissal of the Akhaten religion as merely 'a nice story' clashes noticeably with his famous assertion that 'we're all stories in the end'[105]. In an era so deeply concerned with metafiction, the Doctor's attitude here ought to unsettle us slightly, and smacks of prejudice on his part[106]. The religion of Akhaten is dismissed not because it is a story, but because it is a story from a culture different to the Doctor's own, and therefore implicitly of lesser value. That the Doctor is able to make this assertion, apparently unaware of the contradiction, should strike us as profoundly un-**Doctor Who**. If it doesn't, it is potentially because these imperialist assumptions are deeply embedded in the show's worldview. By engaging with these assumptions, The Rings of Akhaten sets itself a profound task within the context of **Doctor Who**'s history.

---

[104] Anders, Charlie Jane, '**Doctor Who**'s Steven Moffat: The io9 Interview'.
[105] The Big Bang.
[106] Given the reference to 'my granddaughter' in the following scene, the Doctor's attitude here could be read as an inheritance from the more explicitly patriarchal and imperialist first Doctor.

'We're Holding onto Something Precious': The Doctor, Merry, and Childhood in New Atheism

This dismissive attitude towards a supposedly childlike religion also informs the Doctor's treatment of Merry Gejelh. Merry, in fact, is the key to understanding this episode's ideological critique. Through her interactions with the Doctor and Clara we can access the core of the episode's political content, with the Doctor broadly presenting the flaws of New Atheism, and Clara a proposed alternative.

One of the first things we learn about Merry is that she is the 'Queen of Years,' a religious role that means, she tells us, 'I'm the vessel of our history. I know every chronicle, every poem, every legend, every song.' She is an expert in her culture, providing a comparable amount of exposition to the Doctor, and she even demonstrates a degree of genre-savviness. When Clara finishes telling Merry her story of being lost and found as a child, Merry asks, 'And you were never scared again?' – a question prompted by a basic familiarity with storytelling and an ability to anticipate it. When Clara corrects her assumption ('I was scared lots of times, but never of being lost'), Merry smiles as if pleased to have her expectations subverted. As well as being a repository of cultural knowledge, the Queen of Years also plays a central part in the Festival of Offerings the episode centres on.

The Queen of Years appears to be a lifelong position. Merry tells us she was chosen, 'when I was a baby, the day the last Queen of Years died'. This seems to indicate a process of succession not unlike that of the Dalai Lama in the Gelug school of Tibetan Buddhism, with individuals chosen for the role more or less from birth, soon after the death of the previous incumbent, rather than being elected or inheriting the role from immediate family[107]. The apparently lifelong nature of her role means that Merry could, theoretically, have been portrayed as being of any age. Yet when the Doctor and Clara meet her she is, pointedly, a child. This is emphasised by her introduction, as a scared 'little girl' running from patriarchal authority figures, followed by a game of hide-and-seek with Clara. Merry's status as a child may partially explain why the Doctor patronises her throughout the story. He persistently assumes to know more about Merry's culture than she does, giving didactic monologues on the nature of her 'parasite god,' despite the episode's repeated emphasis of his status as a patchily-informed tourist.

This is most blatant during the scene inside the Pyramid. When Clara points out that the Doctor is scaring Merry, he replies: 'Good. She should be scared. She's sacrificing herself, she should know what that means. Do you know what it means, Merry?' Given that Merry is, in fact, an extremely high-ranking member of her religion, it seems unlikely that she wouldn't know what it means. The Doctor, therefore, comes across as patronising and arrogant, taking on the archetypal characteristics of the Orientalist scholar in assuming to explain an ignorant native's own culture back to them, or indeed the New Atheist explaining the childishness of religion.

------

[107] Though the role or even presence of reincarnation in the Akhaten religion is left ambiguous, and the invocation of Tibetan religious traditions on top of the vaguely Middle Eastern iconography further contributes to the episode's Orientalist cultural scramble.

To be fair, the episode does frame Merry as confused and afraid in this moment. An earlier scene even has her admit 'I don't know what to do next.' However, this wording emphasises Merry's indecision as much as her ignorance, and, crucially, **she still knows more than the Doctor**. She knows to expect the Vigil to appear once she refuses to be sacrificed, while the Doctor is left cluelessly asking, 'what's the Vigil?'. Most importantly, it is Merry's knowledge, and not the Doctor's, which enables them to escape the Pyramid. With some prompting from Clara, Merry recalls a folk tale ('The Thief of the Temple and the Nimmer's Door'). The tale includes 'a secret song,' which Merry sings to open a secret door out of the Pyramid. This not only demonstrates Merry's knowledge of her culture, it lends that culture concrete power; its fairy tale magic actually works. In this context, the Doctor's ham-fisted interventions are more a hindrance than a help.

It should be stressed, however, that the Doctor is not wrong to intervene within the episode. He and Clara save Merry from being fed to Grandfather, and their combined actions do eventually save the day. Moreover, the episode clearly frames the Doctor's intentions as noble, making 'we don't walk away' into a tangible heroic moment. (Though note how the line's second appearance, with the qualification that 'when we're holding onto something precious, we run' subtly objectifies Merry). But by intervening in such a patronising, high-handed, and brazenly ignorant fashion, the Doctor actively makes the situation worse. By the same token, it is not that the New Atheists are wrong to oppose religious oppression; it is that their methods of doing so often serve to alienate the very people most affected by it. Both, ultimately, are counterproductive.

The Doctor's assumption that Merry somehow doesn't know the tenets of her own religion also keys into a specific and troubling New Atheist idea. In addition to its infantilising view of religion generally, a recurrent New Atheist motif is that religion is something children cannot, or should not, participate in. The more extreme versions of this argument state, as Dee Amy-Chinn puts it, 'that the inculcation of religion is a form of child abuse'[108]. Dennett points out that, while many religious people consider a child's right to life sacred, 'No child has a right to freedom from indoctrination. Shouldn't we change that?'[109] Hitchens goes further, arguing that religion 'uses the innocent [...] for the purposes of experiment', and that 'the conscription of the unprotected child [...] is something that even the most dedicated secularist can safely describe as a sin'[110].

But of all the New Atheists, Dawkins is most preoccupied with this point. Like his colleagues, Dawkins views religion principally as a set of (incorrect) factual propositions about the material world. As such, he expresses abject horror at the very idea of a religious child. Take this passage from *The God Delusion*:

> 'At Christmas-time one year my daily newspaper, the *Independent*, was looking for a seasonal image and found a heart-warmingly ecumenical one at a school nativity play. The Three Wise Men were played by, as the caption glowingly said, Shadbreet (a Sikh), Musharaff (a Muslim) and Adele (a Christian), all aged four.

---

[108] Amy-Chinn, 'Davies, Dawkins, and Deus ex TARDIS', p32.
[109] Dennett, *Breaking the Spell*, p326.
[110] Hitchens, *God is Not Great*, pp51-52.

'Charming? Heart-warming? No, it is not, it is neither; it is grotesque [...] To see this, imagine an identical photograph, with the caption changed as follows: "Shadbreet (a Keynesian), Musharaff (a Monetarist), and Adele (a Marxist), all aged four." Wouldn't this be a candidate for irate letters of protest? It certainly should be.'

This argument is troubling for a few reasons. Firstly, there's the obnoxious spectacle of Dawkins presuming to understand these children's lives better than they do. More broadly, there is the unexamined assumption that children are incapable of any kind of religious, political, or spiritual engagement, and need protecting from such things. Dawkins argues that:

'Small children are too young to decide their views on the origin of the cosmos, of life and of morals. The very sound of the phrase "Christian child" or "Muslim child" should grate like fingernails on a blackboard.'[111]

Dawkins returns to this theme in his 2019 book *Outgrowing God: A Beginner's Guide*. Explicitly aimed at younger readers, the book is co-dedicated to 'all young people when they're old enough to decide for themselves'[112]. Despite the book's goal of encouraging young people to 'grow up and give up on all gods,'[113] Dawkins maintains that even this decision should be made once a child reaches maturity. Early in the book, he states:

---

[111] Dawkins, *The God Delusion*, pp379-81.
[112] Dawkins, Richard, *Outgrowing God: A Beginner's Guide*, front matter.
[113] Dawkins, *Outgrowing God*, p278.

'One of my pet peeves is the habit of labelling young children with the religion of their parents: "Catholic child", "Protestant child", "Muslim child" [...] It seems to me as absurd as talking about a "Socialist child" or "Conservative child", and nobody would ever use a phrase like that. I don't think we should talk about "atheist children" either.'[114]

While the basic desire to avoid thrusting potentially unwanted beliefs on children is admirable, Dawkins' argument is both misguided about the nature of religious identity and naive about the political context in which children exist. For one thing, Dawkins misses the ways religions operate as social groups. As theologian Nicholas Lash points out, 'To be a Jew, or a Christian, or a Muslim, is to be a member of a particular **people**: a people whose identity is specified by particular habits of memory and ritual'[115] (emphasis his). This is a widely understood concept of religious identity, yet Dawkins' view of religion as primarily a set of positive propositions one can simply agree or disagree with (hence the comparisons to political ideologies) causes him to miss it.

More damningly, it causes him to miss the ways religious groups are racialised. Religious identity frequently overlaps with ethnic and national identities, with all the political implications thereof. Kundnani points out that for Muslims in particular,

'Cultural tropes such as wearing a hijab have come to serve as 21st-century racial signifiers, functioning in ways analogous to the more familiar racial markers of "color, hair

---

[114] Dawkins, *Outgrowing God*, p11.
[115] Lash, Nicholas, 'Where Does *The God Delusion* Come From?', *New Blackfriars*, Volume 80, Issue 1017, p511.

and bone" that WEB Du Bois identified.'[116]

Muslim children in the West often face bullying and discrimination based on their religion[117], and those doing the bullying do not care about their victims' beliefs about the Quran; they care that they belong to a racialised Other. Dawkins' argument does nothing to alleviate this problem. Rather, it potentially exacerbates it, seeking to erase religious identities based on the arbitrary detail of the ages of those being discriminated against. It is an attempt to deal with religious problems, but one harmful to those who feel their worst consequences. A similar dynamic is at work in *The Rings of Akhaten*; the Doctor assumes Merry's ignorance and exacerbates the danger by refusing to listen to her, even though she is the person best positioned to advise him on the problems at hand.

Again, this attitude stands in marked contrast to the Doctor's behaviour elsewhere in the Moffat era. *The Eleventh Hour* sees him actively listening to the young Amelia Pond, to learn about and fix the crack in her wall. Indeed, when we first meet Amelia she is praying to Santa, and the Doctor's arrival is framed as cosmic serendipity in answer to her prayer. In *Night Terrors* (2011) the Doctor explicitly responds to a prayer-like request from a young boy, George, who contacts him by clasping his hands together and whispering 'please save me from the monsters'. In neither episode are these quasi-religious impulses attacked by the Doctor, and in

---

[116] Kundnani, *The Muslims are Coming!*, p58.
[117] Spencer, Caleb, 'Islamophobia: The Muslim Family who "Ran Away" After Abuse'; Haidrani, Salma, 'Islamophobic Bullying Made School a Nightmare'; 'Religious Hate Crimes: Rise in Offences Recorded by Police'.

both instances he actively tries to understand the worldview of the children he interacts with. This fits with the 11th Doctor's broader affinity with children, and the Moffat era's use of children to provide moral perspective. *A Christmas Carol* (2010), for example, has the Doctor's psychic paper 'short out' at the notion that he is 'a mature and responsible adult', and the climax hinges on the young Kazran's horror at his adult self. The Doctor is similarly allied with children in *The Doctor, the Widow and the Wardrobe* (2012), and *The Day of the Doctor* (2013) has him haunted by the children on Gallifrey[118]. All of which makes his high-handed attitude to Merry and her culture even more glaring.

This comes to a head at the episode's false climax, where the Doctor attempts to defeat the Old God single-handed, having shunned the input of both Merry and Clara out of a paternalistic desire to keep them safe. His method of doing so, with a lengthy speech about the Old God's monstrousness and an offering of his own memories, strongly echoes the rhetoric of New Atheism. As we have seen, the Doctor's exclamation that 'You're not a God! You're just a parasite!' parallels a comparison made by Daniel Dennett. In calling the Old God 'eaten out with jealousy and envy and longing for the lives of others,' he echoes Dawkins' description of God as 'jealous and proud of it; a petty, unjust, unforgiving control-freak'[119]. Even the injunction, 'Take my memories,' recreates the basic gesture of New Atheism; that religion can be refuted with sheer empiricism. But as well as its New Atheist inflections, it is worth noting that this speech is, in fact, a false climax.

---

[118] Whose red robes bear a passing resemblance to Merry's.
[119] Dawkins, *The God Delusion*, p51.

'You Have It All!': The Doctor's Speech as Rejected Ending

The second draft of the script for *The Rings of Akhaten* ended with the Doctor giving 'a big speech to defeat the vampire planet'[120]. This was apparently enough to send the Old God packing, and the transmitted ending did not appear until the third and final draft before the pre-production readthrough[121]. According to Cross, this change was made at the behest of Steven Moffat: 'He was really keen that Clara should save the day' rather than the Doctor. What we have in the Doctor's speech, therefore, is not only a 'New Atheist' resolution, but one explicitly rejected, by both the episode and its makers.

This raises the question of why it was rejected. One answer may be that it repeats a well-worn **Doctor Who** trope. Endings where the Doctor confronts a vast cosmic force with stirring rhetoric are fairly common, arguably to the point of cliché. In Cross's account, Moffat rejected the original ending because 'he'd already had the Doctor do this a couple of times: at the end of *The Eleventh Hour* when he faced down the Atraxi, for instance.'[122] But on top of these rhetorical triumphs, moments where the Doctor overwhelms a malevolent force by exposing it to everything he feels, knows, or remembers are also familiar. They are particularly endemic to **Doctor Who** tie-in media, partly because they are useful ways to end short, spectacle-focused stories (such as comic strips and

---

[120] Cross, Neil, quoted in Arnopp, Jason, 'Oh, My Stars!', DWM #464, cover date October 2013, p52.
[121] *The Complete History* Volume 73, p15.
[122] Quoted in Arnopp, 'Oh, My Stars!', p52.

shorter audio dramas), and partly because invocations of **Doctor Who**'s history appeal to the fan-dominated audiences for such media. Eddie Robson's audio *Phobos* (2007), for example, ends with the eighth Doctor defeating a fear-eating alien by feeding it all the things he is afraid of. Leah Moore, John Reppion, and Ben Templesmith's comic *The Whispering Gallery* (2009), meanwhile, sees the 10th Doctor destroy an emotion-consuming monster by exposing it to his own tortured psyche.

Endings like these are thematically interesting, given their emphasis on the Doctor's vulnerability (which Matt Smith seizes on, even shedding a tear at a peak of dramatic intensity). But at the same time, their reliance on the Doctor's troubled past, or indeed his 'secrets that must never be told,' fit comfortably into by-now-typically bombastic depictions of the Doctor as a mythic figure, his vulnerability ultimately making him less human. Given this context, the decision to allow the Doctor this game-ending move, only to deny its usual power, is a solid narrative subversion. As Cross himself says, as a writer, 'one of the great joys is anticipating the twist that you would expect as an audience member, then subverting it and doing something else entirely.'[123]

More pertinently, such a conventional ending would have been a thematically weak conclusion to the preceding story. Merry's leading of the Akhaten choir gives her a nominal involvement in the Doctor's speech, but it would be a frustratingly passive way to follow up the previous scene, which turned on her knowledge and initiative. Furthermore, it would leave Clara with nothing to do, which would be particularly disappointing on her first bona fide

---

[123] Quoted in Arnopp, 'Oh, My Stars!', p50.

adventure.

Indeed, there is something basically unsatisfying about the idea of the Doctor saving this particular day so straightforwardly. As well as being dramatically inert, it would be a strange instance of the master's tools dismantling the master's house. The driving figure of the Akhaten sections of the episode has been Merry, and specifically her liberation from patriarchal institutional structures. The Choristers clearly hold power over her, despite her high-ranking status, and are introduced as trying to coerce her into a religious ceremony she is having doubts about (in stark contrast to Clara, who listens to her concerns and offers encouragement). That Chorister Rezh Baphix is both among Merry's pursuers and the lead singer of the Long Song firmly ties the notion of patriarchal control to the institutional structure of the Sun Singers. At no point do he or any of the other Choristers demonstrate any concern for Merry's well-being, beyond her ability to perform the Long Song. His response to Grandfather waking up, namely to abandon Merry while claiming the Long Song ended with him, is telling. While the episode may reject the paternalism of New Atheism as embodied by the Doctor, it also rejects the oppressive paternalism of patriarchal religious institutions.

The Doctor's speech is thus inadequate as a solution to the episode's dramatic concerns because the Doctor, like New Atheism, is insufficient to the task of combating religious oppression. While he is undeniably opposed to this religious patriarchy, he is opposed to it primarily **because it is religious**, rather than because it is patriarchal. As the episode repeatedly points out, there is a similarity between the Doctor and the Old God – they are both, after all, sometimes known as Grandfather. This is stressed by the otherwise gratuitous mention of Susan earlier in the episode, and cemented when Merry tells us that, if the ceremony fails, Grandfather will 'spread across the system, consuming the Seven Worlds. And when there's no more to eat, he'll embark on a new odyssey among the stars.' The threatened 'odyssey among the stars' is a clear parallel with the Doctor's own wandering lifestyle, though in this context Grandfather becoming more Doctor-like is a thing of cosmic horror rather than a great spirit of adventure[124].

Metatextually, the notion of Grandfather feeding on stories reflects Steven Moffat's own longstanding attitudes to **Doctor Who**. Frank Cottrell-Boyce recalls being advised by Moffat that '**Doctor Who** gobbles up stories. You give it your best film idea and it'll use it in half an hour.'[125] This reiterates a view Moffat expresses in a 2007 episode of **Doctor Who Confidential**:

> 'you know you've got a good idea for a **Doctor Who** story if you think, "Well I've just blown that feature film idea forever, haven't I?" That's the size of story that gets you through 45 minutes of **Doctor Who**.'[126]

---

[124] Here *The Rings of Akhaten* fits within a broader trend in 21st-century **Doctor Who**, whereby the nature of the Doctor and his behaviour is played for horror. The 11th Doctor in particular is frequently compared with ancient and callous cosmic forces. The antagonist of *The God Complex* (2011), for example, describes him as 'An ancient creature, drenched in the blood of the innocent, drifting in space through an endless, shifting maze.'

[125] Quoted in Sproull, Patrick, 'Frank Cottrell Boyce: "There Are a Lot of Similarities Between *Chitty Chitty Bang Bang* and **Doctor Who**."'

[126] **Doctor Who Confidential**: *Do You Remember The First Time?*

Given this view of **Doctor Who**, the decision to make the villain of *The Rings of Akhaten* a story-consuming entity feels provocative. Grandfather's status as a long-lived being with legions of admirers invites comparisons with **Doctor Who** as an institution, as well as the Doctor's diegetic status as someone who has 'lived a long life and [...] seen a few things.' The Doctor cannot defeat Grandfather because the two are aligned at a fundamental level. This is not a moral equivalence, nor is it the dreary trope whereby the hero and villain ostentatiously mirror each other[127]. It is simply that the Doctor, due to the limits of his perspective on Akhaten, and his own similarities to the monster exploiting it, is unable to offer a compelling alternative. The Doctor cannot defeat the evil patriarchal god, because he is himself inextricably patriarchal, at least within this story.

Or rather, he can't defeat it alone. It is notable that both Moffat and Cottrell-Boyce frame writing for **Doctor Who** in terms of sacrifice, of 'using up' their best ideas. While the Doctor tells the Old God to 'take my memories,' there is nothing to suggest he actually forgets his own past here. It is not enough to simply offer memories; one must give up some future potential, deny oneself the benefits of a material object. The Doctor's speech is a failure because he sacrifices nothing in giving it.

This is why the plot is ultimately resolved, not by the Doctor, but by Clara Oswald, and her sacrifice of 'the most important leaf in

---

(2007).

[127] As seen in Cross' own **Luther**, where archvillain Alice Morgan asserts that the difference between her and John Luther is 'one of degree, not category.' (**Luther**, Series 1, Episode 2 (2010)).

human history'. In doing so, Clara not only rescues the Doctor and saves the day. She also participates in the rituals of Akhaten's religion, collaborates with Merry Gejelh, and begins to articulate an alternative worldview in the face of the Doctor's limiting cultural imperialism.

CHAPTER 2: CLARA, MERRY, AND THE MOST IMPORTANT LEAF IN HUMAN HISTORY

Given that *The Rings of Akhaten* concludes the Doctor is inadequate to the task of saving the day, and needs to be bailed out by Clara, it is worth examining her role in the story in more detail. Compared with the Doctor, Clara displays a noticeably different attitude towards Akhaten and its inhabitants. This is partly due to her relative inexperience, and a function of the episode's status as a 'companion's first trip' story. But even with this context, it is remarkable how much of the episode hinges on Clara's relationship to the setting. In contrast to the Doctor, Clara is more curious about Akhaten, more respectful of its culture, more willing and better able to participate in it.

The crux of this, and indeed the entire story, is her relationship with Merry. This chapter therefore focuses on their surprising similarities – they are both young women with a deep investment in storytelling, caught up in patriarchal systems – and how these similarities are built upon to form a cross-cultural collaboration against the patriarchal worldview embodied by Grandfather. It also explores the nature of Clara's final sacrifice, and how her leaf helps symbolically undermine the Doctor's patriarchal and imperialistic attitudes (albeit imperfectly). Moreover, it argues that this act marks Clara's ultimate embrace of, and participation in, the culture of Akhaten, cementing her heroic position within **Doctor Who**.

Places to See: Clara's First Trip

Before we get to Clara's role in the climax, it is worth examining her actions in the story up to that point. The first time we see Clara as an adult in this episode, she is sitting on the stairs holding her book, *101 Places to See*. Jenna Coleman's acting in this 16-second scene is instructive; her restless, tapping finger indicates impatience for adventure, and her broad smile at the doorbell ringing signals pleasure at its arrival. This is a fairly archetypal set of attributes for a **Doctor Who** companion (albeit complicated by the context of the previous episode, as we know Clara has delayed this gratification), and this small scene is a fairly conventional set of actions for such a character.

It is worth asking, therefore, what this scene is doing in the episode. The fact that the Doctor has picked up Clara to take her travelling is communicated by the following scene in the TARDIS. The pre-credits sequence with a solo Doctor could easily establish the timeline, and, if not, a line about the Doctor picking up Clara could have been dubbed in. The decision to film Clara sitting in the hallway was a deliberate production choice, executed relatively late. The bulk of filming for *The Rings of Akhaten* took place between 22 October and 6 November 2012, with most of the pick-up shoots taking place on 12 and 15 November. This scene, however, was filmed on 30 November, significantly later than most of the rest of the episode, and 'on a mock-up set [...] by a double-bank unit under John Hayes and Stephen Woolfenden'[128]. Why did the production team go to the trouble of shooting this relatively lightweight scene, almost a month later and under a different set of directors?

The most straightforward answer is logistical. Without this scene,

---

[128] *The Complete History* Volume 73, p25.

there is no indication that Clara brings her copy of *101 Places to See* with her to Akhaten. While both the book and the leaf feature in *The Bells of Saint John* (2013), the idea that Clara would take them to Akhaten is far from obvious. The episode's climax, however, hinges on Clara having the book (and its contents) with her. Given that, in Cross' words, 'The leaf only became Clara's tool of triumph on the third draft'[129], it seems reasonable to assume that this scene was filmed late in production to establish the presence of an important plot device.

However, while this scene does serve a strict plot function, it also serves a character function. Put simply, it **matters** that Clara Oswald is the sort of person who takes a beloved childhood book with her on her first space adventure. Clara's interest in stories and culture (and the metafictional qualities which will define her tenure) are firmly in play here. We can see that Clara's copy of *101 Places to See* contains several bookmarks, implying extensive reading and selection of favourite passages. This indicates a depth of thought about the book, and, along with her fondness for the book *Summer Falls* in *The Bells of Saint John*[130], about literature in general. The book's title, and the globe on its front cover, help reinforce Clara's interest in travel, and underline her excitement at getting to travel herself. In bringing the book on her first TARDIS trip, we can read Clara as beginning a conscious fusion of travel and literature, which carries over into the following scene aboard the TARDIS.

Asked to choose a destination from all of time and space, Clara

---

129 Quoted in Arnopp, 'Oh, My Stars!', p52.
130 To the point of having a favourite chapter, and a cheekily metafictional one at that.

frames her indecision in literary terms: 'You know when someone asks you what's your favourite book and straight away you forget every single book that you've ever read?' This line is interesting partly because it frames TARDIS travel as a choice among pre-existing texts (which, of course, it is). But it also stresses an intensely personal relationship to those texts, establishing the episode's initial tone of childlike wonder, and introducing the thematically important concept of memory. Yet the Doctor, in this scene, is oblivious to Clara's analogy. He responds, 'No. Totally not,' to Clara's book comparison, then impatiently asks, 'And? Back to the question?' If Clara is already beginning, in the words of Caitlin Smith, to deploy her 'love of storybook tropes' to enact a 'transformation from her "perfect" mask to her "hero" one'[131], the Doctor is hopelessly behind.

Clara's eventual request for 'something awesome' further contributes to the scene's tone of childlike wonder, and highlights her suitability to the role of **Doctor Who** companion[132]. Her first reaction to Akhaten (an awestruck 'It's...') conforms to this pattern of desire, cementing her initiation as companion. Cross describes the deliberately slower pace of these early scenes as a choice to 'give Clara some time to look at things through wide eyes.'[133] It is

---

[131] Smith, Caitlin, 'Masked', in Sastim, Defne, and Caitlin Smith, eds, *101 Claras to See*.

[132] In the Moffat era, the companions' capacity for wonder is an explicit reason the Doctor takes them on. The 11th Doctor explains to Amy: 'After a while, you just can't see it. [...] But you, you can see it, and when you see it, I see it.' (**Doctor Who**: The Complete Fifth Series – 'Additional Scene' (2010)).

[133] Quoted in Arnopp, 'Oh, My Stars!', p53.

worth mentioning that this desire for spectacle aligns with the dehumanising aspects of Orientalism discussed in Chapter 1. Said points out that in European accounts, 'the vision of Orient as spectacle, or **tableau vivant**' consistently recurs, contributing to a framework whereby 'the Orient is **for** the European observer'[134]. The depiction of Akhaten as an awesome spectacle first and a place where people actually live second chimes with these dehumanising patterns in Western scholarship and fiction[135], although within **Doctor Who** this issue is far from unique to *The Rings of Akhaten*.

Yet even at this stage, there are hints, though qualified and ambiguous, that Clara has a deeper interest in Akhaten and its culture. Upon being shown the Pyramid and told about the Sun Singers, Clara asks 'Can we see it? Up close?' This is easily read as a desire for further spectacle; Clara asks to 'see it' (the planet), rather than to 'meet them' or even 'see them' (the planet's inhabitants and/or the Sun Singers). But on the other hand, this line suggests a desire to learn more about the area, and it is Clara who initiates further contact with Akhaten[136].

One of Clara's first questions upon entering the Tiaanamaat market is, 'What do I call them?' The Doctor answers by rattling off a list of

---

[134] Said, *Orientalism*, p158.

[135] Though there were plans at the script stage to feature Akhaten's inhabitants before the arrival of the Doctor and Clara, they were not realised in the final episode (*The Complete History* Volume 73, p13).

[136] Compare this to Amy in *The Beast Below* (2010), who accepts the Doctor's declaration that 'I never get involved in the affairs of other peoples or planets,' until he initiates contact with Starship UK.

species names, but the question's phrasing is ambiguous; it could be interpreted as an inquiry about proper terms of address, which would enable Clara to talk to the locals directly. This willingness to talk carries into the encounter with Dor'een, where Clara, after some initial nerves, gamely attempts to bark back, and receives an encouraging, if untranslated, response. Clara also displays curiosity about the planet's system of currency, and although she makes a negative value judgement ('That's horrible'), her basic interest in the culture remains.

At this point, two very important things happen. First, the Doctor briefly exits the story, spending roughly the next seven minutes off-screen, and offering no explanation on his return. His absence necessarily weights this stretch of the episode. Without the Doctor, the audience has nowhere to look but at Clara. This allows us to learn more about her as a character, and helps the episode to earn its final substitution of her heroism for the Doctor's. Because the second important thing that happens here is the introduction of Merry Gejelh.

Impossible Girls?: Clara and Merry

From their very first encounter, Clara acts as an ally to Merry. When Merry runs into her, Clara's first reaction is to ask if she is OK. When Merry runs off, Clara refuses to help the pursuing Choristers, then follows Merry herself. This is a clear, if one-sided, act of support, and places Clara firmly in a heroic mould. Indeed, travelling to an alien world and intervening to help a distressed little girl is precisely what the Doctor does in *The Beast Below* (2010), the last solo companion 'first trip' story. The pattern's recurrence here serves both to differentiate Clara from Amy, and to emphasise that Clara is taking on some of the Doctor's usual functions for this section of the episode. Her Doctorishness continues in the following scene, as she persuades Merry to trust her and leads her away from the Vigil. All of this contributes to an emerging sense of Clara as a Doctor-like figure. Steven Moffat comments that, 'When I first wrote Clara, I thought, "Oh, this is fun. If the Doctor were a young woman living in contemporary Britain, it'd be a bit like her."'[137]

But while Clara's behaviour is broadly Doctor-like, the details are sharply differentiating, at least in *The Rings of Akhaten*[138]. Part of this is Clara's inexperience — she tells Merry 'I've never been anywhere like here before,' whereas the Doctor has explicitly visited Akhaten previously — and part of it is symbolic. After leading Merry away from the Vigil, Clara is barred from re-entering the TARDIS, as if she has not yet earned free rein over **Doctor Who**'s world. But on top of these structural factors, there is a more basic difference between our two leads: whereas the Doctor initially treats Merry with condescension, Clara listens to her from the start. This is emphasised by the blocking and directorial choices. When the Doctor delivers his 'supernova' speech to Merry later in the episode, he is at first bent over, dominating the frame — literally talking down to her. While Smith does make use of his favoured technique of 'craning his body forward... head slightly lowered so that his eyes are raised upwards to peer into the face of his fellow actor'[139], he returns to a doubled-over posture towards the end of

---

[137] Anderson, Kyle, 'Steven Moffat On Clara Becoming the Doctor in **Doctor Who** Series 8'.

[138] Later episodes will deliberately blur the lines between Clara and the Doctor, to the point where the two are explicitly hybridised.

[139] Hewett, Richard, 'Who is Matt Smith? Performing the Doctor', in

his speech, and maintains a dominant rhetorical style throughout.

When Clara and Merry have their first substantial conversation, sitting together behind the TARDIS, the framing is markedly different. The blocking has both actors sitting down, de-emphasising height difference and allowing a face-to-face conversation. The dialogue largely runs in shot-reverse-shot, with Clara aligned to the left and Merry to the right. But an early shot of Clara and Merry talking face-to-face within the same frame helps establish the scene as a mutually-trusting exchange between equals. It is during this combined shot that Clara admits her own ignorance, asking Merry, 'Could you pretend I'm totally a space alien and explain?' This builds on her earlier admittance that 'I've got no idea who you might be,' and helps avoid any implication of Clara forcefully interrogating Merry. Instead, she patiently listens to Merry's explanation of her predicament, and shows respect for her knowledge of Akhaten's culture. When Merry says that she knows 'every chronicle, every poem, every legend, every song,' Clara is visibly impressed: 'Every single one? Blimey. I hated history.' The overriding tone is one of mutual respect, and it is from this basis that Clara is able to build her own kind of heroic action, as distinct from the Doctor's[140].

Unlike the Doctor, Clara's lack of knowledge about Akhaten does not prevent her from productively helping Merry. While Merry possesses a great deal of knowledge about the local culture and history, Clara is able to offer guidance based on her greater level of

---

O'Day, ed, *The Eleventh Hour*, pp21-22.
[140] It probably helps that Clara has experience caring for children, as established in *The Bells of Saint John*.

life experience. Specifically, she offers Merry a story about her mother:

MERRY

I'm really scared.

CLARA

Everyone's scared when they're little. I used to be terrified of getting lost. Used to have nightmares about it. And then I got lost. Blackpool beach, Bank holiday Monday, about ten billion people. I was about six. My worst nightmare come true.

MERRY

What happened?

CLARA

The world ended. My heart broke. And then my mum found me. We had fish and chips, and she drove me home and she tucked me up and she told me a story.

[FLASHBACK]

ELLIE

It doesn't matter where you are, in the jungle, or the desert, or on the moon. However lost you may feel, you'll never really be lost. Not really. Because I will always be here, and I will always come and find you. Every single time.

Jane Campbell notes the appropriateness of Clara's story here, given its focus on a 'traumatic childhood event,' now 'more or less healed, thanks to her mother'. Clara deploys the story of her own traumatic loss of control to help Merry work through a similar predicament. In doing so, she recreates the support she received as a child. Campbell notes that Clara 'even claims her mother's words: "Oh my stars!"' later in the episode, further establishing Clara's heroism as an iteration of the support provided by her mother. This is a type of heroism we rarely see from the Doctor, given the overt focus on familial relationships, though the episode explicitly reminds us of the Doctor's own family with the early reference to 'my granddaughter'. This suggests Clara's actions as something the Doctor is capable of, even if he has not done anything like this in a long time.

But while Clara's response to Merry's predicament draws on her mother's support, she does not become a straightforwardly maternal figure. Indeed, she resembles Merry far more than her mother in this scene. Campbell argues that 'Merry's desire for perfection is a reflection of Clara's control issues'[141]. Certainly Clara's story, despite its confessional tone, still demonstrates a degree of narrative control. This is most evident in the detail Clara leaves out, i.e. her mother's death. Ellie's declaration that 'I will always be here,' is touching in part because we know it is not true, having learned of Ellie's death within the first three minutes of the episode. Jenna Coleman's downcast eyes and melancholic smile help reinforce the sense that this story might be as much for Clara's benefit as Merry's. Taking control of her childhood narrative helps Clara take control of her situation in the present; it is after relaying this story that Clara asks Merry, 'So, this special song. What are you scared of, exactly?'

---

[141] Campbell, Jane, 'The Circle in the Square (**Doctor Who**)'.

This marks the most important aspect of the conversation between Clara and Merry. Where the Doctor offers a patriarchal rationalism and protectiveness, Clara connects with Merry through a moment of shared vulnerability. Farren Blackburn describes this scene as 'a moment where Clara recounts her fears to Merry [...] I told Jenna, "Try and take yourself back to your own childhood, and put yourself in Merry's shoes."' Blackburn and Coleman consciously worked to establish this sense of camaraderie between Clara and Merry:

> 'I discussed this with Jenna quite a bit: we wanted her to try and embody a kind of "big sister" figure for Merry. Because that's essentially what Clara does [...] It was very much a big sister rather than a maternal kind of relationship.'[142]

Clara and Merry's sisterly relationship chimes with the broader concept of sisterhood in feminist theory. Feminist theorist Robin Morgan argues for a global approach to feminist struggle, because she believes all women share a common world view, 'the result of a **common condition**'[143] (emphasis hers) which she argues all women experience. According to Morgan, all women 'must play essentially the same role, albeit with different sets and costumes'[144], and should therefore understand themselves as 'sisters,' united as a political group by 'the shared, primary oppression of being female

---

[142] See Appendix 2.

[143] Morgan, Robin, 'Introduction: Planetary Feminism – The Politics of the 21st Century', in Morgan, Robin, ed, *Sisterhood is Global: The International Women's Movement Anthology*, p4.

[144] Morgan, Robin, 'Introduction: The Women's Revolution', in Morgan, Robin, ed, *Sisterhood is Powerful: An Anthology of Writings from the Women's Liberation Movement*, pxviii.

in a patriarchal world'[145].

Morgan first formulated this concept in the 1970s, and it has since been widely criticised, particularly by postcolonial feminists[146]. Chandra Talpade Mohanty, for instance, views Morgan's essentialist view of shared female oppression as ahistorical, failing to account for 'particular imperial histories or the role of monopoly capital in different countries'. Mohanty argues that Morgan suggests 'transcendence rather than engagement is the model for future social change', and that this has 'dangerous implications for women who do not and cannot speak from a location of white, Western, middle-class privilege'[147].

Nevertheless, the concept of sisterhood remains important within contemporary feminism, albeit significantly revised, and is applicable to Clara and Merry's relationship in these scenes. In Morgan's view, sisterhood is at least as affective as it is rational, with the theory of women's liberation coming 'out of feeling, not out of textbook rhetoric'[148]. It is from such a basis that Clara and Merry create a strong emotional bond, sealed when Merry hugs Clara at the scene's conclusion. If The Rings of Akhaten is concerned with the problems of patriarchal and imperialistic ideologies, such as New Atheism, in dealing with the traumas inflicted by religious

---

[145] Morgan, 'Introduction: The Women's Revolution', pxxxv.
[146] Morgan has also been widely criticised for her transphobia. Her formulation of sisterhood is not one that includes trans women, and she infamously attempted to have transgender folk singer Beth Elliott expelled from the 1973 West Coast Lesbian Conference.
[147] Mohanty, Chandra Talpade, Feminism Without Borders: Decolonizing Theory, Practicing Solidarity, pp111-12.
[148] Morgan, 'Introduction: The Women's Revolution', pxviii.

institutions, then this scene goes some way towards suggesting an alternative model. It is a model defined by storytelling from a base position of mutual respect and vulnerability, creating the kind of cross-cultural bond that New Atheism and Orientalism implicitly reject.

This model develops further as the episode progresses, and Clara and Merry's relationship moves from mutual encouragement to a more active collaboration. Merry looks to Clara for reassurance before beginning the Long Song, and though she turns on Clara after being dragged to the Pyramid ('You said I wouldn't get it wrong, and then I got it wrong!'), she later runs to embrace her while the Doctor holds off the Vigil. As discussed, it is Merry's cultural knowledge which enables our heroes to escape the Pyramid, but equally remarkable is Clara's instinct to ask her in the first place: 'You know all the stories. You must know if there's another way out.' Clara's respect for Merry's knowledge here facilitates a key plot development, solidifying their trusting relationship. But their most important moment of collaboration comes at the episode's climax; or rather, climaxes. Charged by the Doctor to protect Merry while he deals with Grandfather, Clara returns her to the amphitheatre where she first sang the Long Song. Looking back to the planet, Merry simply says 'I want to help.' Clara responds: 'So do I.' The two women resolve to assist the Doctor, and in doing so help defeat the evil manifestation of a patriarchal system.

This brings us back to the concept of sisterhood. Prominent black feminist bell hooks is among those who argue that Morgan's formulation of sisterhood, based on what hooks calls 'shared victimization', is ultimately limiting. This is partly because it required women 'to conceive of themselves as "victims" in order to feel that feminist movement was relevant to their lives'. Some women, hooks argues, particularly 'those who are exploited and oppressed daily... cannot afford to see themselves solely as "victims" because their survival depends on continued exercise of whatever personal powers they possess'. She therefore advocates a model of sisterhood in which women bond, not through common oppression, but 'on the basis of shared strengths and resources.'[149] Activist Bernice Johnson Reagon is also sceptical of the prevailing conception of sisterhood, and argues for a pooling of resources rather than bonding over victimisation. Reagon, however, favours the rubric of coalition rather than sisterhood: 'wherever women gather together it is not necessarily nurturing. It is coalition building'[150].

This shift from ahistorical sisterly bonding to a more pragmatic politics of solidarity can be read in the development of Clara and Merry's relationship over the course of *The Rings of Akhaten*. Reagon's pronouncement that 'In a coalition you have to give, and it is different from your home'[151] rings true with Clara's sacrifice, and her subsequent observation that her own home 'looks different' to how it did before. But more importantly, the framing of Clara and Merry as both sisters and coalition-builders helps contextualise their collaboration at the story's climax(es). As Mohanty argues, 'For Reagon, cross-cultural, old-age perspectives

---

[149] hooks, *Feminist Theory*, p45.
[150] Reagon, Bernice Johnson, 'Coalition Politics: Turning the Century', in Smith, Barbara, ed, *Home Girls: A Black Feminist Anthology*, p362.
[151] Reagon, 'Coalition Politics', p359.

are founded on humility, the gradual chipping away of our assumed, often ethnocentric centers of self/other definitions'[152]. It is Clara's humility, and receptiveness to Merry's perspective, rather than the Doctor's crass paternalism, which gives Merry the courage to take up the Long Song again.

Because, while Clara may help facilitate it, the following sequence belongs unambiguously to Merry Gejelh. Campbell highlights this as a personal achievement: 'Merry sings a song to Grandfather – **perfectly**. We can tell from Merry's expression that she's nailed it'[153]. What's more, this song marks a clear progression from Merry's previous attempt at the Long Song. The first and second versions of the song, named on the Series 7 soundtrack CD as 'God of Akhaten' and 'The Long Song,' respectively, differ in ways which contribute to this character shift.

'God of Akhaten,' the version used before Merry is kidnapped by Grandfather, remains in the key of A major throughout, and follows an A, D, E chord progression. 'The Long Song,' on the other hand, which begins after Merry returns to the amphitheatre and concludes with the end of the Doctor's speech, is decidedly more complex. The song begins, like 'God of Akhaten,' in the A major key, and moves into F sharp minor, the relative minor key of A major, during the chorus: 'Live, wake up, wake up'. The introduction of minor chords lends the song a heightened gravity, the more sombre-sounding chorus befitting the heightened stakes of this scene compared to the placid religious ceremony of 'God of Akhaten'.

---

[152] Mohanty, *Feminism Without Borders*, p119.
[153] Campbell, 'The Circle in the Square'.

As the Doctor's speech reaches the declaration that he watched until there was 'No time. No space. Just me!' the vocals of 'The Long Song' move from clearly-enunciated lyrics to wordless vocalising. The music shifts from the key of F sharp minor, modulating in a rapid progression between a number of keys until a final B major chord brings the song back into F sharp minor. The vocals return to the phrase 'Cling to your bones / Wake up, wake up,' as the Doctor shouts 'Take it all, baby! Have it! You have it all!'. This musical upheaval helps underline the emotional intensity of the scene, with the Doctor's speech becoming more bombastic as the music rapidly shifts tone, until the return to F sharp minor at the speech's conclusion marks a triumphant return to stability. This stability will of course be undermined by subsequent plot developments, and 'The Long Song' mirrors this subversion with an interrupted cadence, the song ending on a D major chord, rather than the A major or F sharp minor which might be expected given the song's primary key.

The lyrical changes between 'God of Akhaten' and 'The Long Song' are equally important. While 'God of Akhaten' emphasises stillness and rest ('Sleep now eternal. Sleep, my precious king'), befitting its status as 'a lullaby without end,' 'The Long Song' starts with that motif, before quickly abandoning it. Its opening lines, 'Rest now, my warrior / Rest now, your hardship is over,' quickly give way to 'Live / Wake up, wake up'. 'Waking up' is the overriding motif of 'The Long Song'; the precise opposite of 'God of Akhaten'.

There is a narrative reason for this. Not only is Grandfather waking, Chorister Rezh Baphix has explicitly told us that 'the [old] song is over'. Merry is not continuing the Long Song; she is singing a new version of it. The lyrics' move from 'rest now' to 'wake up' enacts

Merry's own movement from passivity to activity, creating a continuity with the previous Long Song before rejecting its stillness in favour of a joyful awakening. Indeed, this new version of the song could be seen as enacting a broader reformation, or even revolution, within the religion of Akhaten. The male religious leaders have fled, so Merry takes the lead in a decidedly new form of worship, the assembled choir following her lead as opposed to hers and Rezh Baphix's.

Yet the new Long Song, joyful as it is, also injects a note of ambivalence. Aside from 'waking up,' its most prominent image is curiously mixed: 'And let the cloak of life cling to your bones / Cling to your bones'. At first this seems a straightforward celebration: a call to accept the warming quality of life and community[154]. Yet the notion of life 'cling[ing] to your bones' is oddly sinister, the phrase's repetition reminding us that Grandfather has been a distinctly acquisitive god up to now. The cloak of life will not let its adherents go, even when they have been reduced, or objectified, as 'bones'.

The slight undermining of the scene's overall tone may be a result of collaborators not being on the same page. Cross' script did not specify any lyrics for the Long Song[155], so these lines were written by composer Murray Gold, perhaps accounting for the tonal deviation. Yet their mildly sinister imagery reflects a larger ambivalence within both versions of the Long Song. Farren Blackburn describes working on the first version of the Long Song:

'In truth, what the Long Song is, is a lullaby. So we had to do

---

[154] Not unlike the use of 'The Old Rugged Cross' in *Gridlock*.
[155] *The Complete History* Volume 73, p17.

our **Doctor Who** version of a lullaby, not all sort of warm and fluffy and cutesy, but something that has believably kept the Old God in slumber for time immemorial. But it also needed to have that slight undercurrent of darkness, that suggested something Other, and foreshadowed some of the danger there would be if the Old God woke.'[156]

This sense of darkness is more explicit in the second version of the Long Song, emphasising the sense of continuity, and subtly hinting that Akhaten's religious revival may not be as straightforward as the song's joyful tone suggests. While musicologist Vasco Hexel is on largely firm ground when he says 'There is nothing subtle about Gold's scores'[157], the lyrics here do sound a cautious note in a song otherwise filled with ecstatic rebirth.

But while Gold's lyrics may slightly undermine the sense of renewal, his composition overall remains characteristically bombastic, and 'The Long Song' sequence generally feels triumphant. This is an appropriate tone for Merry, who enters the story unsure of her ability to sing the Long Song, and leaves it not only capable of singing it, but of rewriting and improving it. Triumph is also an appropriate note for Clara and Merry's relationship. Campbell notes that, as Merry sings, 'Clara's expression is one of complete approval'[158], and this moment can be read as a validation of their collaboration and solidarity. The only person for whom triumph seems an inappropriate emotion in this scene is the Doctor, who

---

156 See Appendix 2.
157 Hexel, Vasco, 'Silence Won't Fall: Murray Gold's Music in the Steven Moffat Era', in O'Day, ed, *The Eleventh Hour*, p173.
158 Campbell, 'The Circle in the Square'.

fails to defeat Grandfather. Yet the sheer uplifting power of the music in this sequence is almost enough to make the Doctor's speech a satisfying climax in spite of itself.

Almost. Neither the accomplishments listed by the Doctor nor visibly achieved by Merry are enough in themselves to defeat the Old God. It takes Clara, and her memory of her mother, to realise the solution. The Old God desires a sacrifice. So Clara must not only fulfil this desire, but subvert it; she must embody the story of her mother by being present precisely through absence.

Now, this development does raise a problem. Given that Clara's actions in this story have been heavily influenced by her collaboration with Merry, the fact that she makes the final, day-saving move alone feels unsatisfying. Merry's dropping out of the story here feels like a missed opportunity, which sells short much of the episode's thematic and political work in building up her relationship with Clara. (The implications of this choice will be dealt with in Chapter 3.) Merry's absence aside, the scene in which Clara sacrifices her parents' leaf is the highlight of the episode, creating a satisfying emotional catharsis where the Doctor's epic speech fails, and cementing Clara's position as a hero.

A Leaf Out of Clara's Book: Narrative Sacrifice

It may help at this point to look at Clara's own speech to the Old God, in contrast to the Doctor's. As well as being shorter and less bombastic, its delivery is significantly different. Jenna Coleman speaks in a lower register throughout, maintaining a quieter and more even tone than Matt Smith. Yet both actors visibly shed tears as the Old God's tendrils reach out to them, implying a significant overlap in their emotional states. Clara's sacrifice may be of a different, more successful, type, but the two characters are trying to achieve the same basic ends. According to Farren Blackburn,

> 'Even though [Smith and Coleman] have two very distinct speeches, they have their own moments within that scene, in a way we treated the whole scene as one performance they were sharing [...] Jenna was a spectator throughout Matt's speech. I think she would freely admit that watching the level of emotion that he reached really helped her gauge where she needed to step in.'[159]

With this in mind, the text of Clara's speech is worth examining:

> 'Still hungry? Well, I brought something for you. This. The most important leaf in human history. The most important leaf in human history. It's full of stories, full of history. And full of a future that never got lived. Days that should have been that never were. Passed on to me. This leaf isn't just the past, it's a whole future that never happened. There are billions and millions of unlived days for every day we live. An infinity. All the days that never came. And these are all my mum's.'

First of all, we have the idea of sacrifice ('I brought something for you'). Having already sacrificed her mother's ring in the effort to save Merry, Clara realises that the only way to defeat Grandfather is with a correspondingly larger sacrifice. Specifically, that of the most important leaf in human history. The phrase's repetition here serves the same purpose that the phrases 'every single time,' or 'wake up' do elsewhere in the story. They act as maxims, incantations, self-

---

[159] See Appendix 2.

reassurances; in other words, stories.

In her review of *The Rings of Akhaten*, science fiction author and critic Charlie Jane Anders takes issue with Clara's leaf being used to defeat Grandfather. She argues that 'It only really works if you think the parasite god has never encountered the concept of death before'. On the face of it, this is a reasonable criticism. If we read the climax as the Old God being defeated simply by 'Clara's grief over her mother's death'[160], as embodied in the leaf, it does implausibly suggest that none of the millions of objects sacrificed previously have ever been associated with dead loved ones. It also raises an uncomfortable imperialist implication, wherein Clara saves the people of Akhaten by doing something they are quite capable of themselves.

But this argument misses the other half of Clara's speech. Clara acknowledges that the leaf is a sacrifice like any other in the Festival of Offerings; it is 'Full of stories, full of history'; imbued with sentimental value. But it is also 'full of a future that never got lived'; full of unfulfilled potential. It is this unfulfilled potential, this space where stories could have been, or 'should have been' as the Doctor puts it, that allows Clara to defeat Grandfather. Where finite stories could be easily consumed, the infinite negative space of possibility is overwhelming[161].

---

[160] Anders, Charlie Jane, '**Doctor Who**'s New Companion Is Only Lovable When the Show Isn't Trying to Make Us Love Her'.

[161] In contrast, the consumption of unfulfilled future potential is the modus operandi of the Weeping Angels, who thrive on this kind of negative space. That the Angels can readily consume something which kills the 'Old God' of Akhaten puts something of a dent in its

Defeating a God that feeds on memory with an object symbolising the unrealised future is a canny role-reversal, but more important is who decides that the leaf represents the future: Clara herself. As a companion, Clara is often associated with the act of storytelling. Kevin Burnard calls her an 'Egomaniac Needy Storyteller'[162], while Caitlin Smith argues that in *The Rings of Akhaten* Clara reveals 'not only how much she enjoys being the hero (complete with a deus ex machina), but also how much meaning she can give an ordinary object with the power of her determination'[163]. Clara defeats the Old God not only by sacrificing a symbol of her past, but by framing it as simultaneously representing an infinite, never-to-be-realised future; by telling a story about it. It is this realisation, and this seizing of the initiative, which enables Clara to defeat Grandfather and save the day, to rewrite her own past and create a better future from the infinite potential of fiction.

Clara's ability to seize control of **Doctor Who**'s narrative by narrativising herself is a core aspect of her character. Her willingness to continually rewrite herself to become the show's hero will strongly define the rest of her tenure. Indeed, according to Elizabeth Sandifer, by the end of Series 9, **Doctor Who** is 'Clara's show now; she's just graciously permitting the Doctor to continue appearing in it'[164]. *The Rings of Akhaten* marks the beginning of this

---

divine status, and the implicit connection between Clara and the Angels raises theological implications beyond the scope of this book.

[162] Burnard, Kevin, 'Egomaniac Needy Storytelller', in Sastim and Smith, eds, *101 Claras to See*.

[163] Smith, 'Masked'.

[164] Sandifer, Elizabeth, 'Impossible Girl (*Hell Bent*)'.

three-season character arc. It is the first time we see Clara[165] rewrite herself in response to the world of **Doctor Who**[166], and the first time the narrative of **Doctor Who** is consciously rewritten to accommodate her as its hero. The bulk of this arc is beyond the purview of this book, but *The Rings of Akhaten* marks an essential early step in this understanding of Clara as a character.

Clara's leaf also bears a strangely ambivalent relationship to the Festival of Offerings itself. In its status as an offering defined by lack, by the absence of singular narrative, Clara's leaf can be read as a rejoinder to the underlying principles of Orientalism as embodied by the Doctor. Said describes the formation of an Orientalist canon:

> 'Residence in the Orient involves personal experience and personal testimony to a certain extent. Contributions to the library of Orientalism and to its consolidation depend on how experience and testimony get converted from a purely personal document into the enabling codes of Orientalist science.'

Orientalism, according to Said, depends on the 'conversion... of personal sentiments about the Orient into official Orientalist statements'[167]. This is not as simple as saying that personal prejudices are automatically accepted as fact. Rather, Orientalist discourse endows the experience of Western observers with greater scholarly weight than the 'Orientals' themselves, who are

---

[165] Rather than one of her 'pieces'.
[166] Having been at least partially rewritten in *The Bells of Saint John*, where she gains computer hacking abilities after being uploaded to the Great Intelligence's 'data cloud'.
[167] Said, *Orientalism*, p157.

systematically excluded from the production of knowledge about their own regions. Said identifies this logic in Karl Marx's declaration that 'They cannot represent themselves; they must be represented'[168], and we can read the Doctor's speech as a failed attempt to 'represent' the people of Akhaten ('Can you hear them? All these people who've lived in terror of you and your judgement').

Clara, on the other hand, does something subtly different. Not only does she make no claim to 'represent' the people of Akhaten (even while participating in their Festival of Offerings), she explicitly offers Grandfather a symbol of the **absence** of personal experience, transgressing the means by which Orientalism consolidates itself. In doing so, she seizes the episode's ending and the role of hero by paradoxically downplaying her own knowledge of the setting, becoming both bolder and more humble. This is a political and aesthetic alternative to the inadequacies of New Atheism and its Orientalist influences; one based on respect for and learning from other cultures, and a type of heroism based on cross-cultural sisterhood and collaboration.

All of which is somewhat undermined by the episode's final scene, in which the Doctor gives Clara back her mother's ring, saying 'They wanted you to have it [...] All the people you saved.' This closing scene, in fact, is in some ways the most frustrating of the episode. The lack of a final interaction between Clara and Merry is disappointing, and detracts from the importance of their collaboration. Furthermore, what feels like a crucial story beat – the community's reaction to Grandfather's disappearance – is sidelined. There is also the frustration of the Doctor referring to the people of

---

[168] Quoted in Said, *Orientalism*, pxvii.

Akhaten as a nameless 'they,' implicitly 'those people'. He has failed to learn his lesson, and is back to representing nameless others rather than respected individuals. There is a similarity here with the way he fails to start treating Clara as a person from now on, refusing to explain the 'Impossible Girl' mystery and once again passing up help from a woman well positioned to give it.

But while this scene is in some ways the episode's most frustrating, it is also, symbolically, one of the most crucial. Clara, having participated in the Festival of Offerings, and saved the day in doing so, is repaid by having her mother's ring returned to her. This invites a symbolic reading; the return of the ring reinforces the 'I will always come and find you' message of Clara's story, and 'rhymes' thematically with Merry's own proposed sacrifice being undone. More importantly, the episode frames the return of Clara's ring, not merely as a return of lost property, but as a reward; specifically, as repayment. Given the way psychometry works as a system of exchange on Akhaten, whereby 'the more treasured [objects] are, the more value they hold,' what does it mean when the people of Akhaten give Clara her mother's ring? It means that they treasure it enough to give it as payment to someone who has just saved the world. Clara, having learned to appreciate and participate in Akhaten's culture, however obliquely, is repaid in kind; the people of Akhaten attach sentimental value to an object of Clara's, and in returning it to her, they apprehend its full worth.

But, most importantly, this moment reinforces the sense of solidarity between Clara and Akhaten. The Rings of Akhaten are not just clusters of rock in space; they are a culture which Clara encounters, learns about, and (in contrast to the Doctor) participates in on a basis of empathy, trust, and above all, respect.

And because of her ability to empathise with Akhaten on its own terms, she will be wearing one of its rings for the rest of her life.

CHAPTER 3: MARKS OUT OF AKHATEN

As beautiful and potentially liberating as *The Rings of Akhaten*'s aesthetic and political vision is, however, the episode is not entirely without flaw. While this book certainly disputes the claims of some contemporary reviews, and this chapter argues that Cross' wider career may have created unfair expectations, at least some of the episode's poor critical reception can be pinned on muddled storytelling. Similarly, while the episode's politics are surprisingly radical, and chime with much feminist and postcolonial theory, there are also significant shortcomings by those same standards.

This chapter therefore focuses on *The Rings of Akhaten*'s flaws, in terms of both its storytelling and its wider political context. In particular, it examines the episode's relationship to some key concepts in postcolonial and feminist theory, and the ways in which it both exceeds, and tragically fulfils, the expectations of these schools of thought. None of this is to denigrate the episode. It is simply to argue that, while *The Rings of Akhaten* represents a positive step forward for **Doctor Who**, there are several ways in which it could have gone further.

'To Feed the Old God': Problems of Emphasis

The Doctor and Clara sit in the amphitheatre as Merry and Chorister Rezh Baphix lead the Long Song. The Doctor explains that the song is a 'lullaby without end to feed the Old God.' The surrounding locals suddenly lift up their hands. We see one in close-up, holding a small white tube. Clara asks, 'What are they doing?' The Doctor replies, 'These are offerings.' We see another local holding up a bowl of blue crystals, which begins to glow. The Doctor continues, 'Gifts of value. Mementoes to feed the Old God.'

The offerings dissolve into golden fragments and float away. We get a quick close-up of the white tube dissolving, then a wide shot of the amphitheatre with golden light streaming away from the worshippers. We then move swiftly on, as the locals join the Long Song in earnest and Merry is kidnapped.

Many critics cited *The Rings of Akhaten*'s climax as a weak point of the episode, with Clara's leaf sacrifice in particular often criticised as a narrative contrivance. Writing for *Den of Geek*, Simon Brew calls it 'a prolonged, ultimately slightly underwhelming denouement,' in which the villain is defeated 'seemingly comfortably enough'[169]. Mark Snow of *IGN* remarks that 'Saving the day through a heartfelt sing-song and the illogical powers of an emotional leaf felt like a distinct cop-out'. Some of this reaction is likely due to simple dislike of the sentimental tone; Snow memorably calls the Doctor's speech a 'late-on, rushed, emo-splurge'[170]. But a fair proportion of this reaction may be a result of the episode's blink-and-you'll-miss-it setup for a key narrative beat. When Clara defeats Grandfather by sacrificing her leaf, it feels like an unearned contrivance rather than an intuitive ending (at least for some viewers) because the mechanics of offerings were not sufficiently emphasised leading up to this point. Where the setup of offerings described above lasts a grand total of four seconds, Clara's sacrifice of her leaf takes a leisurely 40, significantly longer than all the other sacrifices in the episode put together. The episode de-emphasises a narrative element, namely the mechanics of

---

[169] Brew, Simon, '**Doctor Who** Series 7: *The Rings Of Akhaten* Review'.
[170] Snow, Mark, '**Doctor Who**: *"The Rings of Akhaten"* Review'.

sacrifices, that its conclusion then depends on. It is therefore unsurprising that the conclusion frustrated some viewers.

This is one of a handful of underdeveloped aspects of the episode, many of which centre on either crucial narrative moments (like the climax), or things considered especially important to **Doctor Who**. Monsters, for example, are widely regarded as a core part of the show's appeal, and the comparatively minor role of the Vigil is cited as a failing of the episode. While many reviews praise their visual design – Morgan Jeffrey of *Digital Spy* calls the Vigil 'creepy and imposing'[171] and Dan Martin at *The Guardian* describes them as 'an effective menace' – most go on to lament wasted potential. Martin calls them 'little more than placeholding footsoldiers'[172], while Alasdair Wilkins' review for *The AV Club* argues that 'the Vigil doesn't get a chance to build on their initial creepiness'[173]. Even Farren Blackburn felt the Vigil had untapped potential:

> 'One of the things I really liked, but think was under-used, was actually the Vigil. I think they had a lot of potential, to have a greater impact on the episode, and on Merry's journey as a character, and I think that was a little under-exploited. I slightly regret that, and I wonder, perhaps, if we had the time again, whether we could use the Vigil to greater effect.'[174]

---

[171] Jeffrey, Morgan, '**Doctor Who**: New Episode *The Rings of Akhaten* Review'.
[172] Martin, Dan, '**Doctor Who**: *The Rings of Akhaten* – Series 33, Episode Seven'.
[173] Wilkins, Alasdair, '**Doctor Who**: *The Rings of Akhaten*'.
[174] See Appendix 2.

The Vigil's relationship to Merry is especially pertinent. While the Vigil act as a tool of Grandfather, and by extension the patriarchal religious institutions we spend the episode overthrowing, Merry never quite has a moment of direct confrontation with these forces. Perhaps if she had worked out a way to subdue the Vigil (possibly using the cultural knowledge that helps our heroes escape the Pyramid), it might have better utilised the Vigil as monsters, and helped establish Merry's newfound confidence before she restarts the Long Song. At the very least it might have been more dramatic than the Doctor holding them off with his sonic screwdriver, in one of the episode's more underwhelming moments.

Nevertheless, the relative flatness of the Vigil as antagonists may have been a deliberate choice. Cross' script was influenced by the horror writer HP Lovecraft, whose 'old, alien gods'[175] provided a model for Grandfather: 'I loved the idea of the Doctor facing down one of Lovecraft's Old Gods: an alien so alien that it's practically a supernatural being.'[176] The imposing, unknowable Vigil may be an application of this principle to something that can feasibly menace our heroes within the studio. In creating an imposing monster but refusing to divulge substantial information about them, Cross may be aiming for a version of Lovecraft's otherworldly cosmic horror[177]. To explain the Vigil, or even straightforwardly defeat them, might be to undermine the point.

---

[175] *The Complete History Volume 73*, p15.
[176] Cross, Neil, quoted in Arnopp, 'Oh, My Stars!', p52.
[177] Lovecraft's influence can be felt elsewhere in **Doctor Who**, most notably in the **New Adventures** novels, some of which overtly feature versions of his creations.

But this logic falters in the face of wider patterns within **Doctor Who**[178]. The history and conventions of **Doctor Who** mean audiences are more likely to read a vaguely-characterised threat as 'generic monster' than 'ancient unknowable force'. While the Vigil are unnerving, with their mouthless faces, whispered speech, and ability to throw people around, they come across as well-designed stock characters rather than Lovecraftian beings beyond earthly comprehension. As with many aspects of *The Rings of Akhaten*, audience expectations undercut the subtleties of the episode's construction, and the episode itself sometimes fails to emphasise its most important points.

'Possibly a Touch Embarrassed': Neil Cross and Audience Expectations

On top of the genre expectations of **Doctor Who**, an entirely different set of expectations came attached to the words 'Written by Neil Cross'. *The Rings of Akhaten* was first broadcast in April 2013, after the first two series of Cross' acclaimed crime drama **Luther** (2010 and 2011), with a third series following a few months later in July 2013. By this point, **Luther** (2010-) had received five Primetime Emmy Award nominations[179], including for Writing for a Miniseries or a Movie in 2012[180]. Cross can thus be regarded

---

[178] To say nothing of the problems inherent in copying such an infamously racist author as Lovecraft.

[179] 'Emmy Winners and Nominees 2011: Complete List'; 'Emmy Winners and Nominees 2012: The Complete List'.

[180] Its star, Idris Elba, won the 2012 Golden Globe for Best Performance by an Actor in a Mini-Series or Motion Picture Made for Television. ('Golden Globes 2012: The Winners List').

alongside Richard Curtis, Neil Gaiman, and Frank Cottrell-Boyce as one of the Moffat era's 'celebrity writers'; prestigious names famous for work outside **Doctor Who**, who contributed at least partially due to their own love of the programme[181].

But while Curtis, Gaiman, and Cottrell-Boyce's first **Doctor Who** episodes all bore distinct similarities to their most popular work, *The Rings of Akhaten* bears little resemblance to what a casual viewer in 2013 might associate with Neil Cross. **Luther** is a violent and portentous detective show whose morally ambiguous hero is introduced letting a murderer fall from a great height. *The Rings of Akhaten* is a child-friendly fantasy story where familial attachments ultimately save the day. Or, as Kyle Anderson at *Nerdist* puts it, '**Luther**'s a gritty cop drama about serial killers and corruption and redemption, and this episode is, at its heart, about a little girl who is scared to sing in public.'[182] While Anderson views this tonal difference positively, it is understandable that some viewers found it jarring.

Multiple contemporary reviews, both positive and negative, note the difference between *The Rings of Akhaten* and Cross' most popular television work. Russ Ruediger at *Vulture* enthuses that 'Whatever one might have had in mind based on a familiarity with **Luther**, *The Rings of Akhaten* must surely be 180 degrees in yet another direction.'[183] Graham Kibble-White at *Doctor Who Magazine* (DWM), meanwhile, introduces Cross as 'creator of the

---

[181] The Chibnall era would continue this tradition with Malorie Blackman in Series 11 (2018).
[182] Anderson, Kyle, '**Doctor Who** Review: *The Rings of Akhaten*'.
[183] Ruediger, Russ, '**Doctor Who** Recap: The Lord and the Rings'.

superb BBC One thriller **Luther**', before lamenting that 'Neil Cross, as he's proven elsewhere, is a great writer. [...] How did it all go wrong?'[184] The two pieces discuss different types of expectations, with Ruediger focusing on content and Kibble-White on quality, but both share an underlying surprise that such an episode could come from this specific writer.

But while *The Rings of Akhaten* is certainly very unlike **Luther**, the tonal differences belie its thematic continuity with Cross' television work before and since. Most of this continuity centres on the planet Akhaten, as the association of villainy with astronomical bodies is a recurring motif for Cross. In the very first episode of **Luther**, archvillain and femme fatale Alice Morgan is established as a PhD in astrophysics, and she later describes a photograph of a black hole:

> 'This is a black hole. It consumes matter, sucks it in – crushes it beyond existence. When I first heard that, I thought, that's evil at its most pure. Something that drags you in, crushes you, makes you nothing.'[185]

This strongly echoes Akhaten's modus operandi, though the Old God is more cruel in specifically destroying that which is most precious to its acolytes.

Alice's description of a black hole is repeated almost verbatim in the second series of **Luther**. While speculating on a serial killer's plans, John Luther declares, 'Cameron is the opposite of a bomb right now. He's about silence, emptiness, and absence. [...] The opposite of an explosion is an implosion. Black hole.' He elaborates:

---

[184] Kibble-White, '*The Rings of Akhaten*', p64.
[185] **Luther**, Series 1, Episode 1 (2010).

'A black hole consumes matter and crushes it beyond existence. When I first heard that, I thought, that's evil at its most pure, isn't it? Something that drags you in and crushes you to nothing.'

This repetition serves to underline Luther's increasing closeness to Alice Morgan's outlook, with the attendant moral ambiguity, and would be enough to establish black holes and a degree of cosmic horror as a recurring theme for Cross. But the rest of this scene forges a tangible symbolic connection between **Luther** and *The Rings of Akhaten*. John Luther continues:

'Who do we love the most? Who do we protect, who do we shield from all the evils of the world? Who do we lie to, leave them terrified in the dark? Who do we tell that there is no such thing as the Bogeyman? I think that Cameron is going for the children.'[186]

John Luther's mission for the rest of the episode is to protect a set of children from this symbolic 'black hole'. In writing a **Doctor Who** episode about protecting a child from an evil cosmic entity that seeks to reduce her to nothing, Cross can be read as recreating this plotline in a more literal manner (as well as one suitable for children to actually watch).

This sense of cosmic horror is present in **Luther**'s later series, even years after *The Rings of Akhaten*. In Series 5, Episode 2 (2019) Alice Morgan tells John Luther:

'Did you know the observable universe got bigger? [...] Last

---

[186] **Luther**, Series 2, Episode 2 (2011).

tIme I saw you, we assumed there were about 200 billion galaxies. The revised estimate puts it at two trillion, so what we believed to be absolutely everything was basically just a rounding error. Closer to zero than the true number.'[187]

The horror has evolved from being reduced to nothing to the sheer vastness of the universe, a move not unlike Grandfather's consumption of everything followed by an odyssey among the stars.

The uncanny nature of the universe is also touched on in Cross' MR James adaptation *Whistle and I'll Come to You* (2010). The protagonist, played by John Hurt, at one point reflects on his wife's dementia: 'The universe is usually so parsimonious, conservation of energy and so on. But not when it comes to love. When it comes to love the universe is oddly profligate.'

He later makes a point of telling a hotel proprietor that he is an astronomer, as opposed to an astrologer. The image of the rational man confronting an irrational universe is common to much horror fiction, and has obvious parallels with the Doctor in *The Rings of Akhaten*. The plot of *Whistle and I'll Come to You* also centres on a lost ring, strangely anticipating that of Clara's mother.

These themes carry over into Cross' other **Doctor Who** episode, *Hide* (2013). Written before *The Rings of Akhaten* and broadcast after, the episode opens as a ghost story, but partway through the Doctor takes Clara on a trip through 'the entire life cycle of Earth, birth to death'. She is visibly upset by the experience, asking the Doctor how he can be OK with this, and reflecting that, 'We're all

---

[187] **Luther**, Series 5, Episode 2 (2019).

ghosts to you. We must be nothing.' This neatly ties the idea of cosmic horror to the traditional ghost story, an association strengthened by the reveal that the story's 'ghost' is attempting to escape from a collapsing pocket universe[188].

The story evokes *Whistle and I'll Come to You* in the subsequent scene. When Clara tells empathic psychic Emma that 'everything ends', Emma replies, 'No, not everything. Not love. Not always.' Again Cross contrasts knowledge of a vast, uncaring universe with the idea of human love. This sentiment is not enough to save the protagonist of *Whistle and I'll Come to You*, who is implied to have crucially misunderstood his wife. But, in *Hide*, this line sets up the story's ultimate resolution; that the ostensible monsters were in fact motivated by love. As the Doctor says, 'This isn't a ghost story, it's a love story.'[189] *Hide* is superficially more similar to Cross' other television work, but it shares *The Rings of Akhaten*'s underlying optimism. Both stories evoke cosmic horror, but ultimately reject it in favour of human love, an option Cross sidesteps in his adult-oriented dramas.

Cross' most straightforward engagement with cosmic horror is undoubtedly **Hard Sun** (2018), a detective show about an impending cosmic event wherein the sun will kill everyone on Earth in five years' time. The idea of a malevolent sun has obvious parallels with the sun-like Akhaten, and the emergence of the 'hard sun' at the end of the final episode bears a vague resemblance to

---

[188] The Doctor even calls the story's ostensible monster a 'bogeyman', echoing John Luther's association of villainy with cosmic decay.
[189] *Hide*.

Grandfather's awakening. This series also sees a head-on engagement with religion, as the third and fourth episodes concern a Catholic priest whose duties prevent him from helping the police after a serial killer reveals his plans during confession.

But while *The Rings of Akhaten* has more in common with Cross' other television work than might be expected, it remains something of an outlier. Its difference from the rest of Cross' oeuvre is most visible when compared to his other **Doctor Who** episode. Reviewing *Hide* for *Doctor Who Magazine*, Kibble-White praises the episode for 'play[ing] straight' with ghost story conventions, and argues that it 'transcends Neil Cross' other story'[190].

While both *The Rings of Akhaten* and *Hide* share a sense of optimism unusual to Cross' other writing, *Hide* hews closer in spirit, emphasising death and the hauntological, even if they are ultimately overcome by a sense of love and wonder. *The Rings of Akhaten*, meanwhile, places love and wonder front and centre. Both episodes open with a couple whose lives define the rest of the story; but where *Hide* presents a straightforward scare, *The Rings of Akhaten* has a romantic 'meet–cute'. This directly emotional style is unusual for Cross, and fits less comfortably than *Hide* into the standard **Doctor Who** template. While the difference can easily be read as a pleasant surprise, Cross' name may have created expectations that *The Rings of Akhaten* could not possibly fulfil, and therefore contributed to its rocky reception.

---

[190] Kibble-White, Graham, '*Hide*', DWM #460, cover date June 2013, pp66-67.

'There's Quite a Difference, Isn't There?': The Doctor's Speech and Fan Reception

The issue of audience expectations also affects the Doctor's speech at the episode's false climax. Initial responses to this scene were decidedly mixed. While Alasdair Wilkins enthuses that 'the Doctor's big speech to the god packs a wallop'[191], Kibble-White argues that 'Matt Smith looked strained by the Time Lord's interminable blubbing'[192]. Opinions that the Doctor's speech was overdone or sentimental were common following the episode's transmission. Even Matt Smith was reportedly aware that he risked this reaction, and took steps against it. According to Farren Blackburn,

> 'The thing that Matt was perhaps most concerned about, and I think most actors would have been, was the speech to the planet at the end. I think every actor worries they have the potential to go way over the top, to the point where it almost becomes pantomime. I remember having conversations with Matt where he said, "If it feels too much, you will let me know, won't you?" And I said to him, "Yes, one hundred per cent. This is an incredibly emotional speech, and I think we can go quite a long way with it, but I'm your safety net, and I'll let you know if you're going too far." [...] That allowed him to stop worrying about it, and concentrate on what I think is a really beautiful performance, in terms of the emotional level that he

---

191 Wilkins, '*The Rings of Akhaten*'.
192 Kibble-White, '*The Rings of Akhaten*', p64.

reaches. It's pitched perfectly.'[193]

Prevailing opinion, at least within fandom, has backed up Blackburn. The Doctor's speech to the Old God is noticeably popular among fans, seemingly independent of the episode itself. While *Doctor Who Magazine*'s 50th Anniversary readers' poll placed *The Rings of Akhaten* in the bottom 10 stories of all time, at 233 out of 241[194], the speech to the Old God proved popular on the convention circuit. Both Colin Baker and Paul McGann gave impromptu readings of it at conventions, and fan impressionists on YouTube have re-imagined it with the ninth and 10th Doctors, as well as impersonating Smith's original delivery[195]. Some of these videos have tens of thousands of views, and the official **Doctor Who** YouTube channel's upload of the clip, titled 'Speech to Akhaten | *The Rings of Akhaten* | **Doctor Who**,' has been viewed over 6 million times[196].

On the face of it, this seems like an example of what film and television scholar Brigid Cherry calls the 'notoriously contradictory'[197] nature of fan audiences. The devaluation of *The*

---

[193] See Appendix 2.

[194] Griffiths, Peter, 'The Results In Full!', DWM #474, p63.

[195] Kahn, Chuck, '*The Rings of Akhaten* Read by Colin Baker (Sixth Doctor)'; TheSolarminiteBomb, 'Paul McGann Reads from *The Rings of Akhaten*'; Walsh, Pete, 'Ninth Doctor – *Rings of Akhaten* Speech'; Crossley, Elliott, 'Impression #3.5 – 10th Doctor (*Rings of Akhaten*)'; DantheGlassesMan, 'Matt Smith Impersonation – *Rings of Akhaten* Speech'.

[196] 'Speech to Akhaten | *The Rings of Akhaten* | **Doctor Who**'.

[197] Cherry, Brigid, '"Oh, No, That Won't Do at All…It's Ridiculous!": Observations on the *Doctor Who* Audience', in O'Day, ed, *The Eleventh Hour*, p225.

Rings of Akhaten within *Doctor Who Magazine* coupled with fandom's celebration of the episode's major set piece certainly feels counterintuitive. But as Cherry points out, fandom at large contains multiple 'trajectories of fannishness'[198], with disparate relations to and opinions about the show, coexisting 'sometimes contentiously and problematically.'[199] It is not that the singular entity of **'Doctor Who** Fandom' contradicts itself; but that an identifiable group within fandom dislikes the episode overall, while another values the Doctor's speech as a moment worth celebrating. These groups undoubtedly overlap – one may enjoy the Doctor's speech as a highlight of an otherwise disappointing story – but there are two clearly different impulses at play here, most likely reflecting the values of different groups within fandom.

This may partly be traceable to differences in age. The average voter in *Doctor Who Magazine*'s poll was 33, 'became a *Doctor Who* fan in 1988, and started reading DWM in 1996.'[200] While the age of audiences for individual YouTube videos is hard to determine, the platform's most committed viewers skew young. A 2016 study found that the site's 'Die-Hard' users 'skew towards the Millennial (Age 18-34) demographic'[201], and statistics from 2019 indicate that 81% of US internet users aged 15-25 use YouTube[202]. It is plausible that these videos are watched by a materially different age group to

---

[198] Cherry, '"Oh, No, That Won't Do at All."', p212.
[199] Cherry, '"Oh, No, That Won't Do at All."', p221.
[200] Griffiths, Peter, 'The Data of the Doctor!', DWM #474, p66.
[201] 'What Millennials' YouTube Usage Tells Us about the Future of Video Viewership'.
[202] Clement, J, 'Percentage of US internet users who use YouTube As Of 3rd quarter 2019, By age group'.

the *Doctor Who Magazine* poll respondents (though there is surely some overlap).

The question therefore becomes not, 'Why does fandom dislike the episode but enjoy the Doctor's speech?' but 'What about the Doctor's speech does a certain group within fandom feel is worth celebrating, seemingly independent of the episode itself?' Journalist Matthew Hurd describes the appeal of this moment in a 2013 *WhatCulture* piece:

> 'For the first time in a long time, we see the Doctor laid bare. He tells the Slumbering God, and by extension the audience: I feel, and this is who I am because of it. Take me if you dare.'[203]

There is vulnerability here, but also swagger, and a degree of machismo. The sentence 'Take me if you dare' adds an aggressive note to this appreciation of the speech; the Doctor's vulnerability is fuel to a pugnacious rhetorical stance. We are invited to enjoy that stance, but not to examine how it proves counterproductive within the story, or how the problem faced is eventually solved.

A pertinent comparison is with the Doctor's equally bombastic speech from *The Pandorica Opens* (2010). Rhetorically, the speeches are similar in structure, with dismissive addresses ('Hello Stonehenge!', 'Oh, you like to think you're a God') giving way to grand declarations about the Doctor (who is 'standing in your way', having 'watched universes freeze and creations burn') before ending with short imperatives to mark a decisive challenge ('Do the

---

[203] Hurd, Matthew, '**Doctor Who**: 10 Reasons *The Rings of Akhaten* Is The Best Episode Since *The Eleventh Hour*'.

smart thing. Let somebody else try first,'[204] 'Take it all, baby! Have it! You have it all!'). More broadly, the two speeches act as cathartic moments in their respective episodes, where the Doctor faces vast, alien adversaries, and proclaims, in effect, 'Come and have a go if you think you're hard enough.'

That such moments prove memorable is not surprising, and nor is the fact that both speeches are adored by fandom. The so-called 'Pandorica Speech' has similarly been performed at conventions, by Sylvester McCoy, Peter Davison, Paul McGann, and Colin Baker[205], and the BBC Studios YouTube upload of the speech has received over 2 million views[206]. This reception, like that of the Akhaten speech, leaves out important context from the original episode. In context, neither speech plays as an unambiguous triumph.

In *The Pandorica Opens*, we learn that the coalition of enemy forces has in fact been in control of the situation all along. The Doctor's speech amounts to empty grandstanding in an always-already-hopeless situation. For *The Rings of Akhaten*, the issues go even deeper. The Doctor overreaches himself in this scene, misunderstanding both the nature of the problem and the means of solving it, and exhausts himself before being bailed out by Clara and her leaf. Far from a heroic triumph, this speech is an unambiguous

---

[204] All quotes not from *The Rings of Akhaten* are from *The Pandorica Opens*.
[205] TARDISkey, '**Doctor Who** – 7th Doctor – Pandorica Speech'; Stylin' Steve, 'Peter Davison reading Matt Smith's Pandorica Speech'; Bean, Brad, 'Paul McGann reads Pandorica speech at Cincinnati Comic Expo'; hbk51385, 'Colin Baker Reads the Pandorica Speech (**Doctor Who**)'.
[206] BBC Studios, '"I. AM. TALKING!" – **Doctor Who** – BBC'.

failure. Yet much of the fan reception seems to value this speech as a moment of triumph in its own right; a status which noticeably does not extend to Clara's subsequent, less flashy words and actions, which actually solve the problem.

It is tempting to read this discrepancy as sexism on the part of fandom and the **Doctor Who** PR machine. But it is difficult to blame audiences for focusing on the Doctor more than Clara here, if for no other reason than that the episode itself does. For all the quiet poignancy and liberatory politics of Clara's sacrifice compared to the Doctor's speech, which character is devoted the most screen time in these scenes? Whose actions fit most smoothly into pre-existing models of 'heroic' behaviour? Who is backed up by bombastic music and a soaring choir? (Typifying Vasco Hexel's point that in 21st-century **Doctor Who**, 'no matter how opaque or mysterious the Doctor's monologues get, music affirms his authority'[207]). The Doctor's pre-eminence within **Doctor Who** as a whole tilts things in his favour even before the episode stacks the deck. Clara's sacrifice is not even entirely her own, as the Doctor talks over the last few moments of the scene, glossing a dramatic beat which should require no further explanation.

For all that the Doctor's actions facilitate a critique of New Atheism, *The Rings of Akhaten* arguably captures the seductive power of its rhetoric too well. The Doctor's speech, like the Dawkins or Hitchens witticisms that freely roam social media, is too easily divorced from its original context, and too easily used to propagate regressive orthodoxies. In all its eloquent, cathartic, shareable power, it arguably does more to undermine the story than any other aspect

---

[207] Hexel, 'Silence Won't Fall', p166.

of the episode, and so blunts *The Rings of Akhaten*'s impact as a political intervention.

'Hang on!': Casting an Imperial Metaphor

Speaking of blunted impact, the episode's casting may also present a problem, given its political themes. If we are to read *The Rings of Akhaten* as a story concerned with imperialism, the fact that all of the main characters are played by white people is a serious deficiency. The episode features precisely four visible actors who are not white: Chester Durrant and I-kay Agu, who play two of the Choristers; Patricia Dichler, who is among the market browsers and worshippers during the Long Song; and Howard Howell, another background character in the market and amphitheatre. None of these characters have names, or any lines, and none of the actors appear in the closing credits. The episode's status as a story about imperialism is therefore, if not erased, at least significantly complicated.

In presenting a story about imperialist attitudes and postcolonial politics which predominantly features white actors, *The Rings of Akhaten* slots into a long history of such stories within **Doctor Who**. Jack Graham identifies this same dynamic in *The Mutants* (1972), a story which addresses postcolonial politics with a predominantly white cast:

> '*The Mutants* is mostly about white people, despite being "about" how the British Empire (and European empires generally) colonised Africa, exploited Africans, and created racist apartheid systems. In *The Mutants*, even the black

people are, so to speak, played by white people.'[208]

The Rings of Akhaten, like *The Mutants*, may align itself against the worldviews and history of colonialism, but by centring white characters, and casting white actors in the roles of 'colonised' peoples, it fundamentally limits the scope of its critique. The story becomes more abstracted, and the marginal presence of people of colour within it obfuscates the nature of the politics being dealt with[209].

Doctor Who is far from the only offender in this regard. The marginalisation of people of colour in popular culture about fighting white supremacy has often been remarked upon. This effect is prevalent in science fiction and fantasy, where extraterrestrial and supernatural beings are frequently read as metaphors for marginalised people, and especially in works aimed at younger audiences. Writer and educator Darren Chetty identifies this pattern in the **Harry Potter** series:

> 'The books are seen by many as arguing for inclusivity and tolerance, tackling challenging themes such as racial purity and oppression. These themes are explored through fantasy figures such as wizards, giants and elves. At the same time, amongst the teachers and pupils at Hogwarts, there are very

---

[208] Graham, Jack, 'Empires and Metaphors'.

[209] Moffat would later take active steps to promote the presence of people of colour within **Doctor Who**. In 2016, he commented on casting Peal Mackie as Bill Potts: 'We decided that the new companion was going to be non-white, and that was an absolute decision, because we need to do better on that.' ('Moffat on Diversity in **Doctor Who**: "We Must Do Better"').

few people of colour and no clear explanation of why that might be. So a story that has so much to say about racism on an allegorical level at the same time depicts people of colour as marginal without exploring their marginalisation.'

None of this is to diminish the value of metaphor in exploring such issues in fiction. Chetty notes that the **Harry Potter** approach may have its own benefits, including 'the avoidance of further portrayals of children of colour as victims'[210]. But while *The Rings of Akhaten* avoids unhelpful stereotypes of people of colour as victims, it does so by avoiding depicting them as much of anything. The power and immediacy of its critique are thus limited.

It doesn't help that the episode includes a few unreconstructed stereotypes. One background character, visible in the market and at the Festival of Offerings, is clearly played by a white actor in stereotypical 'Geisha' makeup and headgear. The group of aliens lounging around a small central column near Dor'een's moped stand invokes the common motif of hookah smokers in much 19th-century art depicting 'the Orient'. While these details are mostly confined to the backdrop, their use as visual shorthand to convey Akhaten's 'exotic' nature remains troubling. The episode may criticise the Doctor's imperialist worldview, but it does not justify its own casual use of such racialised imagery, especially given the relative absence of people of colour from the cast. Again, the problem is not with the episode's political inclinations, but that it does not fully commit to its underlying politics.

---

[210] Chetty, Darren, '"You Can't Say That! Stories Have to Be About White People"', in Shukla, Nikesh, ed, *The Good Immigrant*, pp101-02.

'You Don't Know Me?': The Problem of Merry Gejelh

The issue of insufficient political commitment is perhaps most acute around Merry Gejelh. As discussed in Chapter 2, the fact that the episode centres on her relationship with Clara, only to have her drop out before the dénouement, has troubling implications. Merry becomes a launchpad for Clara's heroism, rather than an active participant. She is denied even the relatively passive role of Mandy Tanner in *The Beast Below*, whose tender interaction with the Star Whale prompts Amy to realise its benevolence. Clara's realisation that the Doctor needs her help is prompted by the planet re-expanding and a flashback to the story of her mother, which, while related to Merry, is not actually prompted by any of her actions in the scene. The sacrifice of Clara's leaf is again broadly related to Merry, but plays out with no input from her whatsoever. Merry is ultimately subordinate to Clara, in ways which go beyond the usual subordination of supporting characters in episodes like these. Given that Merry is the cultural representative of a society heavily coded along the lines of historically colonised regions, it is difficult not to read the one as being related to the other.

This chimes with an important current in postcolonial feminism, which is frequently critical of the ways in which Western or 'First World' feminism marginalises colonised or 'Third World' women. Chandra Talpade Mohanty argues that Western feminism historically treated 'womanhood' as a stable, universal category, defined by a 'monolithic notion of patriarchy or male dominance'[211]. This produced a reductive, and ultimately unhelpful view of the 'Average Third World Woman,' whose struggles were essentially the same as those of 'First World' women. Postcolonial theorist Gayatri Chakravorty Spivak calls this dynamic 'the inbuilt colonialism of First World feminism toward the Third.'[212]

The construction by Western feminism of a universal 'womankind,' as distinct from the 'local, contextual analyses'[213] advocated by Mohanty and Spivak, serves to obfuscate the very real power differentials between different groups of women. These critiques lead postcolonial theorist Leela Gandhi to observe that, 'In its more irritable moments [...] postcolonial theory tends to regard liberal feminism as a type of neo-Orientalism'[214]. Women from historically colonised cultures are spoken for by Western liberal feminists, rather than allowed to speak for themselves.

A similar dynamic exists in feminist political organising, according to bell hooks. Despite the fact that 'bourgeois white women liberationists probably know less about grassroots organizing than many poor and working class women', hooks observes that:

> 'Racism allows white women to construct feminist theory and praxis in such a way that it is far removed from anything resembling radical struggle. Racist socialization teaches bourgeois white women to think they are necessarily more capable of leading masses of women than other groups of

[211] Mohanty, *Feminism Without Borders*, p19.
[212] Spivak, Gayatri Chakravorty, 'French Feminism in an International Frame', *Yale French Studies*, No 62, p184.
[213] Mohanty, *Feminism Without Borders*, p36.
[214] Gandhi, Leela, *Postcolonial Theory: A Critical Introduction*, p88.

women. Time and time again, they have shown that they do not want to be part of feminist movement – they want to lead it.'[215]

For these theorists, the formulation of supposedly universal womanhood can act as a smokescreen for the continued domination of privileged white women, even in a politics ostensibly about liberation for all; hooks is blunt in her assessment that divisions between women along class, racial, and cultural lines 'will not be eliminated by [...] romantic reverie about common oppression'[216]. *The Rings of Akhaten*, with its overtly sentimental aesthetic and its creation of a cross-cultural sisterly bond which is ultimately sidelined when our white British heroine takes the lead, can be seen as falling into this pattern of thinking. While Clara and Merry's relationship is both valuable and moving, it is ultimately a vehicle for Clara's character development, over and above Merry's. In this way, the episode reflects a flawed version of 'First World' feminism, in which the 'universal struggle' of womankind obscures the extent to which the empowerment of some is facilitated by the disempowerment of others. As Mohanty puts it, 'Beyond sisterhood there are still racism, colonialism and imperialism'[217].

In failing to follow through on the sisterly bond created between Merry and Clara, *The Rings of Akhaten* relegates much of its 'cross-cultural' work to the realm of the symbolic. Even the final scene, with the Doctor returning Clara's ring rather than any of the locals, serves to further distance our heroes from the world they have

---

[215] hooks, *Feminist Theory*, pp52-53.
[216] hooks, *Feminist Theory*, p44.
[217] Mohanty, *Feminism Without Borders*, p36.

visited. We are presented with the **idea** of Akhaten returning Clara's ring, rather than the act itself. That many of the episode's most important ideas are conveyed through symbolism rather than direct action may be another factor in its reputation as dramatically inert. From a political perspective, it reads as frustratingly timid. But then again, **Doctor Who** has often been a show of incremental progress. If *The Rings of Akhaten* is ultimately less bold and sophisticated than it could have been in dealing with the imperialist and patriarchal assumptions of **Doctor Who**, it deserves at least some credit for engaging with them in the first place. The episode is perhaps best viewed as reformist rather than revolutionary; a useful first step, and one worth celebrating, even if there is much work still to do.

CHAPTER 4: ANNIVERSARY ANXIETY

As well as the histories of New Atheism, colonialism, and feminism, *The Rings of Akhaten*'s broadcast in 2013 positions it as a comment on the history of **Doctor Who** itself, and a surprisingly ambivalent one at that. It shares with many other anniversary stories a sense that **Doctor Who** may be no longer valuable or relevant: an anniversary anxiety. This chapter explores how this anxiety manifests in *The Rings of Akhaten*, and how the story's resolution, with its centring of Clara, represents a distinctly feminine view of the future which underpins Series 7 generally, albeit one with important caveats. Given that some of this future has already been realised, the chapter also examines the ways in which *The Rings of Akhaten* prefigures the late Moffat and early Chibnall eras' active engagement with **Doctor Who**'s history and the role of female characters within it.

'I Know Every Chronicle': Doctor Who and the Anniversary Anxiety

It is useful, in **Doctor Who**, to distinguish between 'anniversary' and 'multi-Doctor' stories, as distinct yet overlapping types of episode. The latter are a well-known quantity. Stories like *The Five Doctors* (1983) or *The Day of the Doctor* are celebrations of **Doctor Who** as both a narrative and a cultural institution, mounted for the special occasion of an important anniversary, and thus openly nostalgic and self-congratulatory. They produce what Matt Hills calls 'feel-good anniversary affects'[218]; fondness for the return of 'the old

---

[218] Hills, Matt, *Doctor Who: The Unfolding Event: Marketing, Merchandising and Mediatizing a Brand Anniversary*, p54.

favourites'[219], and joy at the history and continued existence of **Doctor Who**.

In contrast to these, we have stories like *Snakedance* (1983), *The Greatest Show in the Galaxy* (1988-89), and *The Name of the Doctor* (2013). These stories are also broadcast during anniversary years, and act as commentaries on the series and its past. Indeed, this principle often extends to entire 'anniversary seasons'; Seasons 20 (1983) and 25 (1988-89), as well as Series 7 (2012-13), contain multiple stories that engage with the past of **Doctor Who** in some shape or form. Free of the obligation to provide an elaborate birthday party with a host of returning actors, such stories tend to be more ambivalent about **Doctor Who**. Themes of irrelevance, death, and decay are often foregrounded, and the Doctor is denied some of his usual narrative power. *Snakedance* sees the Doctor trying to warn people about a returning monster only to be ignored; *The Greatest Show in the Galaxy* has him desperately performing for a bored and callous audience; in *The Name of the Doctor* he visits his own grave.

All these stories share a palpable worry that the Doctor, and by extension **Doctor Who**, may be past their prime, on the point of obsolescence or collapse. Even *Silver Nemesis* (1988) has its Iconic **Doctor Who** Monsters fretting that 'The Cyber-race will cease to exist'[220], symbolising the programme's own worries about its material future. (And with good reason, given that its next season would be the last until 2005). These stories exhibit a kind of anniversary anxiety, a sense that **Doctor Who**'s long history, while a

---

[219] *The Day of the Doctor.*
[220] *Silver Nemesis* episode 2.

cause for celebration, may also be a liability: 'We made it this far; but how much further can we really go?' Hills uses the term 'insecure consecration' as a keyword in his discussion of the 50th anniversary's marketing[221], and in these stories that insecurity becomes part of the text itself.

Yet none of these stories are about **Doctor Who** succumbing to the fear of its own irrelevance. They often feature the Doctor learning something new about his past, or being saved from the stultifying grip of history. As such, they serve as demonstrations of what makes **Doctor Who** worth preserving in the first place. *Snakedance* shows the Doctor learning to meditate and overcome the Mara through internal struggle. In *The Name of the Doctor* his friends save him from a 'classic villain,' and *The Time of the Doctor* (2013) has him loudly reject 'the rules of regeneration' to go on living. These stories, while acknowledging the weight of **Doctor Who**'s history, refuse to be bound by it, and conclude with a defiant sense of the show's continued relevance.

This will-to-life is reflected on the symbolic as well as narrative level. Jane Campbell points out the repeated motifs from 'Near Death Experience literature'[222] across Season 20, and argues that the entire season, through an explicitly alchemical process, constructs its own 'arc to infinity'[223]. This symbolic consolidation reflects the brand consolidation that anniversaries represent. Hills points out that, in 2013, 'By commemorating its 50th, *Doctor Who*

---

[221] Hills, *The Unfolding Event*, p27.
[222] Campbell, Jane, 'The Arc of Alchemy (**Doctor Who**: Season 20)'.
[223] Campbell, 'The Arc of Alchemy'.

hence accrues further brand value via emphasising its longevity'[224]. Anniversary anxiety exists to be overcome; these stories act as proving grounds, where **Doctor Who** faces the prospect of irrelevance and articulates reasons for its continued existence.

Which brings us back to *The Rings of Akhaten*, whose engagement with the past is assured. The story opens in 1981, contains an explicit reference to Susan, and lifts iconography from across 20th-century **Doctor Who**, including *The Keys of Marinus*, *Snakedance*[225], and, as Graham Kibble-White points out, *The Pirate Planet* (1978)[226]. But its specific anxiety is rooted in something more basic, which carries through most of Series 7, concerning the very nature of the Doctor as a masculine hero.

'I Have Lived a Long Life': Doctor Who and the Crisis of Heroic Masculinity

To return once again to the Doctor's speech to Grandfather, on top of everything else discussed, it is worth noting the references to previous **Doctor Who** stories. We have by-now standard boasts that he 'walked away from the last Great Time War,' and 'marked the passing of the Time Lords'. But most suggestive is the Doctor's declaration that 'I walked in universes where the laws of physics

---

[224] Hills, Matt, 'Anniversary Adventures in Space and Time: The Changing Faces of **Doctor Who**'s Commemoration', in Hills, Matt, ed, *New Dimensions of Doctor Who: Adventures in Space, Time and Television*, p229.

[225] Whose Manussan bazaar is echoed in the Tiaanamaat market.

[226] At one point we see Clara 'alighting the moped having "just arrived". A trick of *The Pirate Planet* vintage' (Kibble-White, '*The Rings of Akhaten*', p64).

were devised by the mind of a mad man'. The emphasis on the 'mind of a mad man' recalls a number of cerebral Doctor Who villains with reality-building powers, such as the Master of the Land of Fiction in *The Mind Robber* (1968) and Goth in *The Deadly Assassin* (1976)[227]. But most intriguing of all, especially for a story broadcast in an anniversary year, is the applicability of this description to Omega, star of previous anniversary stories *The Three Doctors* (1973) and *Arc of Infinity* (1983), who literally creates his surroundings using the power of his mind. The Doctor is haunted, not simply by his age, but by celebrations of his age. He is aware, not only that he has 'lived a long life' but that he is a hero for having done so.

This is part of a larger pattern of self-awareness within *The Rings of Akhaten*. When Clara asks the Doctor if there is a way out of the Pyramid, he replies, 'Possibly. Probably. There usually seems to be.' This flippant tone masks a basic character trait of the 11th Doctor: he knows he is the hero. He has been in situations like this often enough to trust he will find a way out, and sure enough, he does. Or rather, Clara and Merry find it for him. It is this same self-awareness that leads the Doctor to assert 'souls are made of stories, not atoms,' a statement which, while arguably a crass misreading of Merry's culture, is an entirely accurate assessment of the Doctor. All we know about him, we know through the various narratives he features in; stories are all we have of his soul.

This self-aware heroism also leads the Doctor to declare the soul is made up of 'People we love, people we lost. People we found again against all the odds.' The first sentence points meaningfully towards

---

[227] Both among **Doctor Who**'s more metafictional stories.

113

the story's eventual resolution. The Doctor's narrative awareness leads him to accidentally stumble on the answer, and, in keeping with his behaviour up to this point, he misses it. The second half, however, is more ambiguous. On one level, the Doctor is right that his having found Clara 'against all the odds' is a dead giveaway that he is in a certain type of story. We are even invited to make the Doctor's mistake here, and share in his suspicion that meeting Clara 'out of order' signals some wider deception or plot. But it is, undeniably, a mistake, born out of the Doctor's narrative longevity and heroic self-identity. In retrospect, we know there is nothing sinister about Clara, and that the Doctor did not so much 'find her again' as find the original version of her. Yet his expectations of Clara, like his expectations of Akhaten itself, lead him to make dangerously wrong assumptions; to misread the story he is in.

Which brings us to the spectre haunting all of Series 7: the so-called 'Impossible Girl Arc'. While a full treatment of the arc is beyond the scope of this book, it is safe to say, based on *The Rings of Akhaten*, that the Doctor's initial reactions to the 'mystery' of Clara are driven by his own narrative expectations[228]. Given the overt focus on the history of **Doctor Who** in 2013's 'Series 7B', we can also read them as an expression of anniversary anxiety, here manifesting as a kind of obsessive jealousy.

On a narrative level, the pre-titles sequence for *The Rings of Akhaten*, where the Doctor surveys images of Clara's doppelgängers past and future, before looking at the present day version and

---

[228] This is compounded by the fact that, following Amy's departure, the Doctor decisively becomes the programme's 'viewpoint character' in a way not previously seen in the Moffat era.

exclaiming, 'She's not possible!' sets the tone for a half-series in which the Doctor repeatedly misses the forest for the trees. But if we step back from the immediate dramatic concerns, what do we see? The Doctor is worried that he has met someone who recurs across multiple settings and time periods, and keeps returning despite ostensibly 'dying'. Someone, in other words, who threatens to do as good a job of 'being the Doctor' as he does. That such a prospect is treated as sinister on its face betrays an anxiety about the Doctor's legitimacy that *The Rings of Akhaten* will spend much of its runtime unpacking, and contributes to a seam of self-loathing that has long defined the 11th Doctor[229].

More damningly, though, the fact that the Doctor feels threatened by a woman seeming to do a version of what he does inescapably genders this anxiety. Note the repetition of '**She** can't be! **She** is! **She** can't be! **She**'s not possible!' (emphasis mine) and the fact that Clara's father tells the Doctor 'She wants to be Bryan Robson,' football being another area traditionally dominated by masculine heroes. The Doctor's horror at Clara's recursion is an outgrowth of his narrative expectations, which are themselves the result of an accumulated 50 years of stories in a fundamentally patriarchal paradigm. Not only has he been in enough stories to expect 'a trick' or 'a trap'[230], he is used to being the masculine hero, such that he views a woman ostensibly doing a version of what he does as immediately suspect. The basic misogyny at play here is inescapable.

---

[229] *Amy's Choice* (2010) having established that the person the Doctor hates most in the universe is himself.
[230] *Journey to the Centre of the TARDIS* (2013).

This feeds into a dynamic of the Moffat era, and the Matt Smith years especially, where female companions are made the focus of narrative arcs in ways which objectify them. Dee Amy-Chinn identifies this pattern with Amy: 'while previous companions were central to the resolution of story arcs, Amy **is** the story arc', with the crack in her wall and later her pregnancy forming the central pillars of Series 5 and 6. A similar phenomenon affects Clara in Series 7: she **is** the eponymous 'Impossible Girl' of the series' arc, and, like Amy, her lack of narrative awareness in comparison to the Doctor disempowers her. Amy-Chinn argues that Amy:

> 'embodies the potential danger posed by women – and the fact that she does so unwittingly offers a subtextual agenda of female passivity at odds with a more straightforward reading that puts focus on her agency.'[231]

As with Amy before her, the Doctor consciously withholds information from Clara, deliberately placing her at a narrative disadvantage. This instinctive distrust is exacerbated by the more overtly misogynistic dimensions of the Doctor's behaviour.

Because the other noteworthy thing about the opening is its implication of stalking. The Doctor surreptitiously follows Clara and her parents, and scrolls through images of Clara and her duplicates in a scene that evokes social media stalking. This is one of multiple instances where the viewer is made uncomfortable by the Doctor's 'investigations' of Clara. The aforementioned reference to 'finding her again' has a worryingly predatory undertone, and the episode

---

[231] Amy-Chinn, 'Amy's Boys, River's Man: Generation, Gender and Sexuality in the Moffat Whoniverse', in O'Day, ed, *The Eleventh Hour*, p73.

concludes with a lengthy shot of the Doctor staring darkly after Clara before closing the TARDIS door.

For all their earnest sentiment, the opening scenes have a consistently troubling undercurrent, even when the Doctor is not their focal point. The use of The Specials' song 'Ghost Town' as Dave walks along the road helps establish the period setting, but it also adds a mildly sinister undertone. A similar contrast is established by the Doctor hiding a calculating look behind the *Beano Summer Special*. The heavy rain of the following scene has a similar double signification. On the one hand, couples having intense conversations in the rain has precedent in the romantic comedy genre (*Four Weddings and a Funeral* (1994) being perhaps the most famous example). But on the other, the generally negative connotations of rain, the darkness of the scene, and the ominous rumble of thunder help underline the creepiness of the Doctor watching from afar. His furtive behaviour in the graveyard as he observes the grieving Clara and Dave further adds to the sense of wrongness; the Doctor implicitly disturbs Ellie's peace. The implication of the Doctor as a stalker, then, is not accidental, but an active part of the episode's design. *The Rings of Akhaten* wants us to be aware of the Doctor's suspicion of Clara, and, moreover, wants us to be uneasy about it. We may be invited to share in the Doctor's intrigue at the mystery of Clara, but we are also, to some extent, alienated from it[232].

---

[232] This is admittedly complicated by the treatment of stalking elsewhere in the Moffat era. Jack Graham takes the era to task for its use of the 'stalking-as-romance trope' (Graham, Jack, 'Steven Moffat – A Case For The Prosecution'). While in *The Rings of*

This, then, is the outline of *The Rings of Akhaten*'s anniversary anxiety. The Doctor's long life, in both a literal and a cultural sense, has led him to view Clara with suspicion, at least partially because she threatens to be his equal. 50 years of patriarchal narrative expectations have curdled into a kind of misogynistic jealousy. But this is not a condemnation of the Doctor: it is the starting point for an arc which will resolve this anxiety by addressing these flaws in the Doctor's character. Much of this arc takes place beyond *The Rings of Akhaten*, but the episode does offer a crucial piece of the jigsaw, pointing to the arc's eventual resolution.

'She's Not Possible!': Clara Oswald and the Alternative Resolution

Given the Doctor's implicit fear about Clara supplanting him, the story's resolution, in which she succeeds where he failed to defeat the Old God, would seem like a vindication. The episode asks us to compare the two characters as visions of heroism, and comes down on Clara's side. But it's worth returning once again to that sacrifice of the leaf. Because the thing that allows the leaf to defeat

---

Akhaten the stalking is deliberately uncomfortable and the implication that the Doctor is romantically interested in Clara is downplayed, this is a hard accusation to shrug off in the general case. The most infamous example is *The Doctor, the Widow and the Wardrobe* (2012), in which Madge tells the Doctor that her husband Reg 'always used to follow me home', and that 'He said he'd keep on following me till I married him'. This precedent arguably makes the trope's occurrence in *The Rings of Akhaten* harder to read as a criticism of misogyny, rather than an example of it. It would certainly not be the first time that subversive intentions were hampered by unexamined patriarchal tropes in the Moffat era.

Grandfather is Clara's framing of it as not only 'full of stories, full of history' (as the Doctor previously boasted he was), but 'full of a future that never got lived'. In other words, it is the notion of **unfulfilled potential** which allows Clara to defeat the monstrous embodiment of patriarchy. If we read the Doctor's earlier speech as an expression of anniversary anxiety, then this act presents a resolution. The trick is to focus not on what **Doctor Who** has been in the past, but on what it still has the potential to be in the future. As the Doctor says, 'there's an awful lot of one, but there's an infinity of the other'.

We can even read this resolution as commenting on the need to re-evaluate and move on from the patriarchal nature of past stories, given the Doctor's stressing of the difference 'between what was and what should have been'. **Doctor Who** should have been radical, exciting, and liberational; it frequently wasn't, but the recognition that it ought to have been is the first step towards making it so now, and it is Clara who realises the ability to tell this new version of the old story. It's a thematic resolution so effective it borders on the overly neat; progress is rarely so straightforward, especially in **Doctor Who**. But this is, broadly, the thematic statement made by Series 7B as a whole: that **Doctor Who**, for all its rich and valuable history, must focus on the future while addressing the flaws of its past.

It's a statement underlined by various evocations of *The Rings of Akhaten* later in the 2013 series. *The Name of the Doctor* reiterates that Clara 'blew into this world on a leaf', and reuses footage of Clara's childhood for its opening montage, alongside various clips and callbacks to previous Doctors whom Clara saves. That episode concludes with the Doctor saving Clara from the dream-world of his own history using something, 'Not from my past, [but] from yours'. He sends her the leaf she sacrificed to Grandfather, saying 'This is you, Clara. Everything you were or will be. Take it. You blew into the world on this leaf. Hold tight. It will take you home.'[233] The Doctor has learned the lesson of *The Rings of Akhaten*; he recognises Clara's history is of equal importance to his own, and returns her sacrificed leaf like he returned her mother's ring. In doing so, he demonstrates his own appreciation of the most important leaf in human history, and completes the symbolic return of Clara's gifts to Akhaten.

It's a deliberate and charming symbolic knot that satisfyingly concludes the Doctor's character arc for Series 7B; he has learned to treat Clara as an equal, rather than a puzzle to be solved. As Caitlin Smith puts it, the Doctor accepts 'that the ordinary girl behind the mask is just as, if not more, important than the mask'[234]. That said, the immediate sidelining of this character beat to introduce the War Doctor is more than a little disappointing. As in the last appearance of Clara's leaf, the potential of a feminist motif is undercut by masculine heroics.

The Time of the Doctor marks a culmination of these call-backs to Akhaten, as 'The Long Song' is used to score the Doctor's regeneration scene. The visual parallels between this scene and Clara's leaf sacrifice, which both involve the past disappearing in a whirl of golden light, make this a suitable choice. But the thematic resonance goes deeper. The music accompanies the reappearance of Amy, and the Doctor's declaration that:

---

[233] *The Name of the Doctor*.
[234] Smith, Caitlin, 'The Impossible Girl'.

'We all change, when you think about it. We're all different people all through our lives. And that's okay, that's good, you've got to keep moving, so long as you remember all the people that you used to be.'[235]

This is the final scene of the final episode of **Doctor Who**'s 50th anniversary year, and so marks the resolution of 2013's anniversary anxiety. The Doctor has learned to balance appreciation of the past with the need to 'keep moving' and embrace future potential. Specifically, he has learned it from the women in his life; from Amy Pond and, this year, from Clara Oswald. The answer to the challenge, 'How does **Doctor Who** avoid falling into misogyny, given its long history of storytelling within patriarchal frameworks?' is 'By centring the Doctor's female companions and allowing them equal heroic status to the Doctor'. It's a satisfying resolution to the 50th anniversary anxiety, albeit one that raises problems of its own.

'I Lost... My Mojo'[236]: Doctor Who and the Manic Pixie Dream Girl

A key talking point in discussions of Clara in Series 7 is the trope of the Manic Pixie Dream Girl. Often shortened MPDG, the term was coined by film critic Nathan Rabin in 2007, and refers to a type of female lead prevalent in contemporary romantic comedies. Such characters are outwardly quirky, witty, or otherwise intriguing, yet seemingly exist solely to inspire their insouciant male lovers to self-improvement, displaying little evidence of a life or interests outside of them. Prominent examples include Kirsten Dunst's character in

---

[235] *The Time of the Doctor.*
[236] 'The Bells of Saint John: A Prequel' (2013).

Elizabethtown (2005), Natalie Portman's in *Garden State* (2004), and Zooey Deschanel's in *500 Days of Summer* (2009). The trope has been widely identified as sexist, positioning women as delightfully inspirational to men rather than fully-rounded people in their own right. Rabin describes the Manic Pixie Dream Girl as existing 'solely in the fevered imaginations of sensitive writer-directors to teach broodingly soulful young men to embrace life and its infinite mysteries and adventures'[237]. Which, as Elizabeth Sandifer points out, is uncomfortably close to a description of Clara's role in Series 7B[238].

Anita Sarkeesian describes the MPDG as 'a muse who exists to be the inspiration for the troubled, tortured man.'[239] In viewing Clara as a character who teaches the Doctor how to overcome his anniversary anxiety, are we ultimately casting her as **Doctor Who**'s muse? Someone who, while a friend and comrade to the Doctor, is primarily an inspiration for his heroism, rather than a hero in her own right? After all, it is the Doctor, and not Clara, who deals the final rhetorical blow against Grandfather: 'And infinity's too much. Even for your appetite.' But not, it seems, for the appetite of **Doctor Who**, and its continual reassertion of patriarchal norms.

There are hedges against such a reading, of course. Sandifer points out that Clara deviates from the MPDG as originally formulated. In particular, her assertiveness, and the fact that, in *The Bells of Saint*

---

[237] Rabin, Nathan, 'The Bataan Death March of Whimsy Case File #1: *Elizabethtown*'.
[238] Sandifer, Elizabeth, 'My Mind Will Be Like That of a Child (*The Bells of Saint John*)'.
[239] Sarkeesian, Anita, 'Tropes Vs. Women #1: The Manic Pixie Dream Girl'.

John, 'she makes the Doctor come back the next day... speaks to her unique relationship with [him]'[240]. This beat, alongside Clara's job and relationship with the Maitlands, helps establish Clara as what Amy-Chinn calls 'the girl/woman on top'[241], and cuts against any assertion that her life revolves around the Doctor. Indeed, she forces the Doctor to organise his life around her. *Nightmare in Silver* (2013) establishes that they travel together on Wednesdays, meaning the Doctor takes up just one day of her week, rather than being the centre of her life.

Aside from this, the very term 'Manic Pixie Dream Girl' has attracted a fair amount of criticism, to the point where we may question its general utility. Several commentators take issue with the term's over-use, flattening all unconventional female leads into an easily-dismissed stereotype. Monika Bartyzel argues that the term's increasing popularity led to it moving 'from putting a spotlight on questionably hollow female characters to marginalizing and dismissing all manner of diverse female characters on film'. Bartyzel also notes that many so-called 'MPDGs **do** break some genuine ground for female characters', observing that, in some examples, their 'mania' manifests in a refusal to conform to patriarchal standards:

> 'These aren't women written as conforming to peer pressure, adding to the smattering of superficial female characters lacking unique personas [...] Holly Golightly [from *Breakfast at Tiffany's* (1961)] isn't ashamed to be an escort in a world where women are expected to be proper;

---

[240] Sandifer, Elizabeth, 'My Mind Will Be Like That Of A Child'.
[241] Amy-Chinn, 'Amy's Boys, River's Man', p75.

Portman's Sam takes pride in the way she finds humor in life; Deschanel's Summer doesn't care if the outside world thinks she's weird.'[242]

This wave of criticism contributed to Rabin himself disowning the term in 2014. He agreed that it had been over-applied, and concluded by 'apologi[sing] to pop culture: I'm sorry for creating this unstoppable monster'[243].

We might draw an analogy here with another trope from popular media criticism: that of the so-called 'Mary Sue'. Originally coined by fanfiction writer Paula Smith for her 1973 parody fic, 'A Trekkie's Tale,' the character of Mary Sue was meant to send up the idealised 'author-insert' characters prevalent in **Star Trek** fanfiction. Since then, however, the term has undergone a similar drift to the 'Manic Pixie Dream Girl,' becoming a cudgel wielded against any remotely competent or unconventional female lead. Writing about the dismissal of Rey from **Star Wars** as a 'Mary Sue,' Charlie Jane Anders states that the term 'has now become both vague and toxic'. She argues that:

> 'Over time, the term "Mary Sue" has broadened until it means "any female character who is unrealistically talented or skilled." Which is insane for a couple of reasons: It makes this "trope" so vague as to be meaningless, and this is also purely a way at tearing down female characters who are

---

[242] Bartyzel, Monika, 'Girls on Film: Why it's Time to Retire the Term "Manic Pixie Dream Girl"'.
[243] Rabin, Nathan, 'I'm Sorry for Coining the Phrase "Manic Pixie Dream Girl"'.

good at stuff.'[244]

Sophie Collins argues that, in broader discussions about female writers and characters, 'Mary Sue becomes, in my eyes, an unwitting embodiment of the double standard of content'[245]. In this framework, qualities male writers and characters are often praised for become vices once expressed by female ones. While the term 'Manic Pixie Dream Girl' has not been so badly misused as 'Mary Sue,' there is potential for a similar pattern in the description of Clara as a 'Manic Pixie Dream Girl'. She may be a quirky twenty-something who helps coax the Doctor out of an existential malaise and re-embrace a life of adventure, but this is pointedly not the whole of her character.

Moreover, the idea of Clara as a Manic Pixie Dream Girl in her introductory episodes is necessarily complicated by the following two and a half series of further development. The extended runtime of several years' worth of television allows the archetype to be used as a base on which to build a more nuanced, self-actualised character. The observation that Clara fulfils aspects of the MPDG trope in her debut series should be contextualised by her subsequent development into a thrill-seeking adventure addict and immortal time-travelling eccentric. Sandifer argues that 'knowing that she does grow out of [the MPDG trope] highlights the ways in which it never really applied to her'[246]. If Clara is initially positioned as **Doctor Who**'s muse, she is a muse who will

---

[244] Anders, Charlie Jane, 'Please Stop Spreading This Nonsense that Rey From **Star Wars** Is a "Mary Sue"'.
[245] Collins, Sophie, *Who is Mary Sue?*, p27.
[246] Sandifer, Elizabeth, 'My Mind Will Be Like That Of A Child'.

eventually (and decisively) transcend this status.

Nevertheless, initial broadcast viewers of *The Rings of Akhaten* did not have the benefit of two and half years' extra context, and Clara's resemblance to the Manic Pixie Dream Girl cannot be simply dismissed. Amy-Chinn calls the Matt Smith years 'complex and polysemic'[247] in their treatment of gender and sexuality, with liberal attitudes towards gender roles abutting with more conservative impulses like the emphasis on nuclear families. The Impossible Girl Arc is a perfect example of this dynamic in action. Clara is able to become the hero of **Doctor Who**, to the point of 'sav[ing] the Doctor,' but in doing so reiterates harmful tropes about women existing to inspire their partners. It would fall to Series 8 and 9 to move past this problematic dynamic, and indeed to create new problems of their own.

Of course, reading Clara's position in *The Rings of Akhaten* in light of subsequent seasons also demands that we read subsequent seasons in light of *The Rings of Akhaten*. If we are to view Clara as offering a way out of **Doctor Who**'s anniversary anxiety with a vision of infinite, explicitly feminised future potential, it is worth addressing the ways in which some of this future potential has, by now, actually been fulfilled.

'But As Me': Clara Oswald and the Feminine Future

A recent trend in **Doctor Who** criticism treats the late Moffat era's engagement with gender as setting up the Chris Chibnall era, and

---

[247] Amy-Chinn, 'Amy's Boys, River's Man', p84.

the casting of Jodie Whittaker as the first female Doctor. Alyssa Franke closes her book on *Hell Bent* (2015) with the argument that Moffat was 'responsible for laying the groundwork within the show for the Doctor to eventually regenerate into a woman'[248]. Franke highlights Moffat's work 'establishing the continuity within **Doctor Who** that Time Lords could change their gender when they regenerate'[249]. While these arguments often produce worthwhile analysis (Franke is sharp on the changing gender dynamics of the late Moffat years), they sometimes risk falling into teleology. To treat Moffat/Smith/Capaldi solely as the heralds of Chibnall/Whittaker is to cheapen both creative teams, making the former subservient and the latter inevitable. We may also question the emphasis on continuity relative to character and theme. Clara stealing a TARDIS and running away is just as strong a case for a female Doctor as Ken Bones regenerating into T'Nia Miller, if not stronger. As Franke says, by the end of *Hell Bent*, 'there is the sense that if the camera panned to follow the American diner, we might see a television show called "Clara Who" instead'[250].

Moreover, such an argument can be misconstrued as giving Moffat credit for choices he did not make. Franke is correct that, 'In the end, the only decision that mattered was Chibnall's'[251], and we should be cautious of reading one of the most important feminist steps in **Doctor Who** history solely through the lens of the previous regime. Some might argue that 'Moffat walked so Chibnall could run,' but the blunt fact remains that Moffat never actually cast a

---

[248] Franke, Alyssa, *The Black Archive #22: Hell Bent*, p66.
[249] Franke, *Hell Bent*, p72.
[250] Franke, *Hell Bent*, p51.
[251] Franke, *Hell Bent*, p88.

woman as the Doctor. Certainly it is difficult to claim *The Rings of Akhaten* as a secret prelude to the 13th Doctor. While Clara's feminised heroism and the emphasis on sisterhood are welcome and important features, the episode does not necessarily demand that we view the Doctor as potentially female.

That said, there is a material way in which the episode contributes to the build-up to Series 11: through its role in establishing Clara as a character. There are three and a half series between *The Rings of Akhaten* and *The Woman Who Fell to Earth* (2018). Clara stars in two and a half of them, the final one airing after Chibnall was announced as Executive Producer, and she and the 13th Doctor both appear in *Twice Upon a Time* (2017). If any companion has a claim to bridge the gap between Doctors 11 and 13, it's Clara Oswald.

This is true thematically as much as chronologically; the late Smith and Capaldi years continually assert that a woman can take on the role of the Doctor, usually through Clara. *Hide*, *The Day of the Doctor*, and *Listen* (2014) have her piloting the TARDIS. *The Day of the Doctor* and *The Caretaker* (2014) have her close the TARDIS doors by snapping her fingers, which Moffat previously established only the Doctor could do[252]. *Mummy on the Orient Express* (2014) ends with Clara and the Doctor co-piloting the TARDIS, and *Flatline* sees Clara consciously perform the Doctor's role in his absence, prompting him to admit she makes 'an exceptional Doctor'[253]. *Death in Heaven* (2014) sees Clara diegetically impersonating the Doctor to fool some Cybermen, only to be backed up by Jenna

---

[252] *Silence in the Library / Forest of the Dead* (2008).
[253] *Flatline*.

Coleman's name and face taking Peter Capaldi's usual position in the opening titles. And, as previously mentioned, *Hell Bent* concludes with Clara stealing a TARDIS and running away with a companion, in the most unambiguous version of this thematic statement.

These stories do not merely establish that it's possible for Time Lords to change gender when regenerating. They make the pointed statement that a woman can 'be the Doctor,' and fulfil the specific narrative functions associated with that title[254]. Clara is not the only character who does this, of course. Lady Me forms an explicit parallel with the Doctor as a dangerous and untrustworthy immortal in Series 9; River Song continues to be a female action hero in *The Husbands of River Song* (2015); Lucy Fletcher shares the Doctor's knack for sneaking into evil bases and obliviousness to bespectacled superheroes in *The Return of Doctor Mysterio* (2016). And of course Bill, like Clara, ends her story wandering the universe with a new girlfriend in *The Doctor Falls* (2017). But Clara is the most prominent of the Moffat era's proto-female Doctors, and her assumption of the role is the outgrowth of a characterisation which *The Rings of Akhaten* helps establish. This episode is where her affinity with storytelling is made explicit, and her willingness (and ability) to reframe the narrative to her own ends is established.

Again, we should be wary of giving undue credit. Jenna Coleman

---

[254] Which reinforces a broader thematic point of the Moffat era, that 'the Doctor' is less a specific individual than a role the series' central character has created, which anyone can fulfil. Hence his declaration in *Extremis* (2017) that 'you don't have to be real to be the Doctor'.

did not actually play the 13th Doctor, any more than Neil Cross wrote *The Woman Who Fell to Earth*. Those achievements belong squarely to Jodie Whittaker and Chris Chibnall. But the two exist in continuity with one another. *The Rings of Akhaten* is part of the precedent, both thematic and political, upon which Series 11 is based. While Clara in Series 7 helps to resolve the immediate anxiety of the 50th anniversary, she also catalyses broader questions about **Doctor Who**, and is an important player in their development through the 12th Doctor's era, ultimately resolving into that of the 13th (which of course brings its own set of thematic concerns). That is a story worth telling in itself, and *The Rings of Akhaten* stands as a worthwhile precursor; a leaf blown into the face of **Doctor Who**, whose implications we are still exploring.

CONCLUSION

The month of this book's publication marks the seventh anniversary of *The Rings of Akhaten*'s first broadcast. For all that it was dismissed at the time, the intervening years have seen **Doctor Who** repeatedly return to the episode's concerns. Some of this is simply in the ongoing relationship between Clara Oswald and the Doctor, concluding with him finally sacrificing his memories for real, and her running off to see 101 more places, at the end of *Hell Bent*. Part of it is the repeated engagements with imperialist ideology and **Doctor Who** history in stories like *Empress of Mars*, *The Eaters of Light*, and *World Enough and Time / The Doctor Falls* (all 2017). A significant chunk of it is the late Moffat years' emphasis on the power of storytelling, and the ability to rewrite the rules to create better endings, as seen in stories like *Last Christmas* (2015), *Extremis* (2017) and *Twice Upon a Time*.

But the most important engagements have undoubtedly come since 2018, and continue in the still-unfolding Chibnall era. Series 11 saw direct engagements with the history of colonialism and anti-racist struggle in stories like *Rosa* and *Demons of the Punjab*, while *The Witchfinders* and *It Takes You Away* (all 2018) returned to the subject of familial relationships and intergenerational storytelling. Moreover, Series 11 saw a reimagining of the Doctor and her mode of heroism which seems explicitly designed to counteract the character's behaviour in stories like *The Rings of Akhaten*. While the 11th Doctor was quite happy to stroll in with little education and dominate the proceedings, the 13th Doctor seems painfully aware that she doesn't know everything, and is willing to defer to others. As Kelly Connolly puts it:

'Whittaker's Doctor is allowed to not have all the answers; to accept that she cannot be everyone's cure-all; to be curious and authoritative, defensive and empathetic. The Doctor isn't an exceptional woman. The Doctor is a woman.'[255]

This approach is not without its own flaws; that the first female Doctor should be such a non-confrontational hero has unfortunate implications of female passivity. But if nothing else, this characterisation is an effective counter to the Doctor's flaws as portrayed in *The Rings of Akhaten*. It is now harder to imagine the Doctor talking down to Merry Gejelh quite so patronisingly, which is undoubtedly a mark of progress.

On top of this, the programme's relationship to religion has shifted, continuing the Moffat era's slide away from New Atheism. Elizabeth Sandifer notes the 13th Doctor's newfound 'respect for spirituality and religion'[256]. She joins in alien religious ceremonies, speaks of 'my faith', officiates an interfaith wedding, and defends Gloucester Cathedral as 'a place of worship'[257]. Matthew Kilburn argues that, 'though [the Doctor's] faith is defined as personal and beyond denomination, the quasi-sacerdotal role she adopts projects a universalism without seeking to proselytise'[258]. All of which is a far cry from the Doctor's behaviour in *The Rings of Akhaten*; a sign, perhaps, of the character's growth, and certainly of a production

---

[255] Connolly, Kelly, 'The Radical Helplessness of the New **Doctor Who**'.

[256] Sandifer, Elizabeth, '*The Witchfinders* Review'.

[257] *The Tsuranga Conundrum* (2018), *Demons of the Punjab*, *Fugitive of the Judoon* (2020).

[258] Kilburn, Matthew, '**Doctor Who** XXXVII/11.6: *Demons of the Punjab*'.

team taking a more thoughtful view than the New Atheists.

But *The Rings of Akhaten* is not only valuable as a harbinger of things to come. It is a moving, insightful, and beautiful story in its own right, which deserves to be appreciated on its own merits. As an interrogation of New Atheism, it is one of the boldest political interventions in 21st-century **Doctor Who**. As an attempt to create a female-centric version of heroism, it is an early, imperfect step on an important road. And as a story about our power to reshape the limiting, patriarchal narratives in which we find ourselves, it is one of the most powerful in **Doctor Who** history. But on top of all this, for me, *The Rings of Akhaten* will always be a story about learning.

I wasn't always a fan, you see. When I first watched *The Rings of Akhaten*, seven years ago this month, I shared all the complaints this book has examined. It was slow, sentimental, good-looking but hollow. And there it rested for a further three years. In the summer of 2016, I happened to listen to a podcast about the legacy of New Atheism[259]. Having heard it, I innocently fired up *The Rings of Akhaten*, on a whim, and something began to click. I realised, subconsciously at first, that these two things were related. And so began the long process that eventually led to the book you are holding in your hands.

It took me seven years to reach my current understanding of *The Rings of Akhaten*, and I know there's still a lot to learn. This book has made several criticisms of the Doctor's behaviour in this episode; he's pompous, patronising, arrogant, and distrusting. But

---

[259] 'Shabcast 23b: New Atheism is the Opium of Misogynists, Islamophobes, and Imperialists'.

in one respect, he perfectly embodies the spirit of *The Rings of Akhaten*, and that is in his willingness to keep returning. We are told explicitly that he has been here before; we know implicitly that he can come back again. By returning to *The Rings of Akhaten* we can continue to learn about its world, and the things it has to say about ours. It was this process of revisiting that allowed me to turn an unremarkable episode into one of my favourite stories; to turn a dead leaf into a symbol that could pacify a god. For me, learning to love *The Rings of Akhaten* was the key to learning a whole lot more; about **Doctor Who**, about politics, about religion, and about myself. I can only hope that this book helps a few more people learn something, too.

APPENDIX 1: WHAT IS AKHATEN, ANYWAY?

There is some ambiguity about whether Akhaten is meant to be a planet or a sun. On the one hand, as the episode's title suggests, it clearly has rings analogous to the rings of Saturn (albeit some of the asteroids within those rings are significantly larger than the chunks of ice which make up Saturn's). This, combined with the fact that our heroes are able to look at Akhaten without being blinded, would seem to indicate that it is a planet, specifically a gas giant. Official sources back this up, with the *Complete History* partwork referring to 'the planet Akhaten'[260] in its plot synopsis.

On the other hand, Akhaten is routinely read as a sun. In his review for *Nerdist*, Kyle Anderson refers to 'the sun around which the titular rings orbit', and to 'the sun god, which is also called "Grandfather"'[261]. Assumptions that Akhaten is a sun or a star are common in casual discussions of the episode, and as this book shows, not without reason. Chapter 1 discusses Akhaten's resemblance to the Aten, itself a kind of sun deity, and the fact that Akhaten glows orange further adds to this impression.

On a third hand[262], Akhaten also extends glowing tendrils to consume the treasured objects of its adoring worshippers. This suggests that conventional names such as 'planet', 'sun', and 'star' may not be entirely adequate. At least one production document suggests a deliberate ambiguity, with Farren Blackburn's Director's

---

[260] *The Complete History* Volume 73, p11.

[261] Anderson, *'The Rings of Akhaten'*.

[262] And surely, in **Doctor Who**, we can allow ourselves a third hand.

Statement describing Tiaanamaat as 'a vibrant melting pot of alien cultures cast in the light from the imposing planet Akhaten.'[263] That Akhaten apparently casts light suggests it is a star, but the document calls it a planet, blurring the distinction, and suggesting an object which is not quite either. The influence of cosmic horror on Cross' writing is discussed in Chapter 3, and the idea that Akhaten might be neither sun nor planet, but an alien life form masquerading as an astronomical body, is compelling.

That said, there seems to be some genuine confusion in the way Akhaten is introduced. The Doctor guides Clara out of the TARDIS, and we see her face bathed in light. The Doctor says: 'Can you feel the light on your eyelids? That is the light of an alien sun.' When Clara opens her eyes she, and the audience, see a large, round glowing object, orbited by a floating rock large enough to be a planet[264]. The assumption that we are looking at a sun is therefore understandable. This is compounded when the Doctor counts down to the reveal of an asteroid housing the 'Pyramid of the Rings of Akhaten'. He then talks of 'Seven worlds orbiting the same star. All of them sharing a belief that life in the universe originated here, on that planet,' and points in a direction that could indicate either Akhaten or the Pyramid asteroid.

It is tempting to read this as a mistake on the part of the programme-makers. This is, after all, the show that confuses constellations with galaxies on a regular basis. But a more interesting reading presents itself when we remember that the Doctor is the one doing the talking. This book argues that the

---

[263] See Appendix 3.
[264] Or a dwarf planet.

Doctor is a flawed observer of Akhaten and its surroundings. He not only fails to remember the words to the Long Song, he apparently does not recognise Akhaten for what it is until too late. Might we read his ambiguous use of astronomical terms as yet another reflection of his imperfect knowledge of this region and its culture?

For clarity's sake, this book assumes that Akhaten is in fact a planet, albeit a vaguely sun-like one with a few eccentric properties. But the ambiguity of the broadcast episode remains fundamental. We cannot know what Akhaten 'truly' is, at least not while we approach it with the totalising literalism of the ill-informed outsider.

APPENDIX 2: INTERVIEW WITH FARREN BLACKBURN

Conducted via Skype, 6 February 2019.

William Shaw: At what stage did you come on board for *The Rings of Akhaten*?

Farren Blackburn: I came on board five or six weeks ahead of when I was due to shoot the episode. It came about because I'd just done **Luther** for Neil Cross[265], and we'd built up a relationship on that show. He said to me that he was going to do some writing for **Doctor Who**, and there was one particular episode that he was quite excited by. And because I'd previously done the 2011 Christmas special [*The Doctor, the Widow and the Wardrobe*], I was very much in favour of **Doctor Who**. So the production team called me to see if I would do another episode. Knowing it was Neil, knowing I would get a chance to kick around some ideas with him, it seemed an opportunity too good to miss, so I said yes. All I knew at the time was that it was set on an alien planet. So I quickly realised that this episode was going to be a challenge because we wanted to achieve a certain level of production value, but I also knew I was going to be shooting an awful lot of greenscreen, which presents its own challenges. At the time I think Steven Moffat said, 'You know, **Doctor Who** is all about aliens, but how many times do you actually go to an alien planet? It's very rare to do that.' Everyone was quite excited by that prospect, and that was certainly something that appealed to me, from a directorial point of view. So I came on board, and it was a standard amount of prep time,

---

[265] Blackburn directed **Luther** Series 3, Episodes 3 and 4 (2013).

around six weeks. The script was a work in progress, and Neil, being Neil, was working on various different things, and I think me coming on board helped him focus. Neil's very collaborative, he has very strong opinions, but he's always willing to listen to others.

WS: What sort of things were you discussing with Neil?

FB: The discussions were all-encompassing really, from the nature of the story, through to character, and how we might imagine this world we wanted to create for the episode. That obviously goes hand in hand with the team at **Doctor Who**, and the concept artists who work with the director and the producers, trying to realise, for example, what the alien planet might look like. When we were talking about the Vigil, for example, we had a lot of discussions about what they might look like. Because I guess, depending on the writer, **Doctor Who** scripts are sometimes very specific when it comes to describing an alien, or a particular location. Whereas some writers just have quite a loose description for those things.

WS: So was this script especially prescriptive in terms of the visuals?

FB: No, it wasn't, actually. If I recall, it would say something like, 'Clara steps out and she sees an alien planet,' and as our discussions became more in-depth, Neil took a lot of the things we'd discussed and started to put more description into the script. It very much came together as a result of that collaboration.

WS: A lot of people compare this episode to **Star Wars** and **Indiana Jones**. Were those conscious influences?

FB: Those were definitely the two main influences, yes, especially with the marketplace populated by the aliens. We wanted to create the kind of energy you feel in the marketplace for an **Indiana Jones** movie. That meant making sure it looked heavily populated with all the different aliens. Quite often what you do when you're trying to make something look busier than it really is, is you condense the frame by shooting on longer lenses, you crush the focal depth so you don't see as much detail, and suddenly five or six people can look like 20 or 30 people. But I didn't want to try and cheat the audience. Given that this episode was designed to be on an alien planet, I wanted people to really get a sense of that. So we just tried to really pack in as many alien designs and costumes as we possibly could. We wanted that real hustle and bustle, the energy you see in **Star Wars** and **Indiana Jones**. That of course made it very challenging to shoot; the amount of times we had to stop and take the top half of an alien's costume off so that they could cool down! All those things seem trivial, but when you've got 30 or 40 people in alien costumes and they all require that, it's a real hitch to production. But yes, **Indiana Jones** and **Star Wars** were definitely the biggest influences.

WS: I suppose the crowdedness of those initial scenes forms a contrast with the later scenes, which are more intimate. Was that a deliberate contrast, and did that present its own challenges?

FB: I'm not sure if that was necessarily a conscious thing, but that certainly is the way the story evolves, with the Doctor and Clara's quest to save Merry. When you have just two or three characters in a scene, it does allow you to really focus on their performances. Obviously all those scenes later between the Doctor and Merry, and Clara and Merry, they are very intimate, it's about building trust between the characters, and ultimately they become very emotive. So for those kind of scenes it definitely pays to have a quieter, less populated set where you can really work with the actors on achieving the level of emotion required. It's a totally different energy to when you've got 40 people in alien costumes and the support network you need around all those people, it's like a football crowd!

WS: In terms of the intimacy of those scenes, what sort of direction did you give Matt Smith, Jenna Coleman, and Emilia Jones?

FB: Well for example, with Emilia Jones, we were very thorough in casting that role. It's a very complicated part, in terms of understanding the nature of the story and all those layers beneath what's on the page. There's a need to balance that emotional vulnerability with a real level of maturity, which is difficult to find in a very young actor. So we were very thorough in our casting. Whether an actor is young, old, middle-aged, I always try to get the most natural performance possible, even in a show like **Doctor Who**. I always try and ground it in a performance, so that you believe this created reality, even though it's sci-fi. I encouraged Emilia to rely on her instinct, to try and keep it as an understated performance. It was my job to remind her where her character was at any given time in terms of the story, and also the kind of emotion that I felt was appropriate for the scene. But you always have to give an actor a root cause for an emotion. It's not good enough to just say, 'You're frightened here,' or, 'You need to be angry,' because there are so many different reasons in life that you could be angry. So I always try and give a root cause to the emotion, so they can understand where it's coming from. Emilia was super smart, so she took that on board, and she was terrific. With Matt, he's just a very gifted actor, and again a very natural actor. I'd worked with him before on the Christmas special, so I had his trust as a director, and that's crucial. It means he feels safe, so he can take risks in his performance knowing that I'm going to pull him back if he's gone too far, or encourage him to take certain things further if I feel that's appropriate. It's just a dialogue of trust, really. It was the same with Jenna. We got on so brilliantly, and she was very keen to be directed, she's also a super smart actress, and this was her big introduction, her first trip to an alien planet, so she really wanted to get it right. We were very forensic with our performances.

WS: *The Rings of Akhaten* is Clara's first trip in the TARDIS, though some episodes had already been filmed. Did you take any steps with Jenna to try and fill that gap between *The Bells of Saint John* and future episodes?

FB: No, not really. Like with Emilia, it was more about reminding her where her character is in the overall scheme of things. In some regards it was about trying to forget what had come before in terms of her shooting schedule. One of the crucial moments of the episode is when she first steps out of the TARDIS and sees the planet. We were keen to make sure that scene had the wide-eyed wonder of a child, the excitement of her character as this world opens up in front of her. So it was really about stripping away any sense of experience that she'd gained with the character before, and saying, 'You're like a child in the biggest sweet shop here, and when you step out that door, you're really not going to believe your eyes.' It's about capturing that kind of innocence, in a way. Which again was incredibly challenging, because obviously all Jenna and Matt were looking at was a green screen. It takes a particularly skilled actor to project that of level of emotion and wonder when the wondrous sight is in no evidence whatsoever at that point of the shoot! But it helped that we'd had those conversations about what the planet would look like. We tried to give them as much information as possible, to see that then play out in front of them.

WS: You mention encouraging actors to take risks, and Matt asking you to rein him in if he went too far. What sort of risks was he worried about?

FB: The thing that Matt was perhaps most concerned about, and I think most actors would have been, was the speech to the planet at the end. I think every actor worries they have the potential to go way over the top, to the point where it almost becomes pantomime. I remember having conversations with Matt where he said, 'If it feels too much, you will let me know, won't you?' And I said to him, 'Yes, one hundred per cent. This is an incredibly emotional speech, and I think we can go quite a long way with it, but I'm your safety net, and I'll let you know if you're going too far.' It goes back to having worked with him before, that he completely trusted me. That allowed him to stop worrying about it, and concentrate on what I think is a really beautiful performance, in terms of the emotional level that he reaches. It's pitched perfectly. So we'll have a discussion about it, about where we think that performance should be pitched, and then he has to go out and somehow reach that point. But he can't do that if he's worrying that it's either going to be a bit flat, or he's going to step too far across the mark. So that trust allows him to just remove all those obstacles from his mind and concentrate on delivering that performance, and I really think he did.

WS: I agree, I think it comes across beautifully. Were there any times when you asked him to scale it back?

FB: There probably will always be times when I go in and say, 'Look,

I don't think you need to give quite as much there.' I have very strong thoughts about what's required in terms of performance, but I don't work in a dictatorial way. I don't say, 'You have to do this,' I enter into a discussion. But again, it helps when you have the trust of an actor. If I asked for something, Matt would always say, 'Yes, great, I can give you that.' He might occasionally say, 'Are you sure? Will it take a bit away if I take my foot off the pedal a little bit?' and I can always say, 'Look, let's try it. If it doesn't feel right, then we'll go again.' That's the beauty of film, that you can try things out. Obviously you've got to have a clear idea of what you want to achieve, you can't just improvise and ad lib, because schedules don't allow for that. But you can say, 'Look, we've got three or four really good takes in the can at this level, so why don't we try something slightly different?' Because if it works, that's an added bonus. So yes, there were times when I asked for changes, but Matt's so gifted, and for me he was a perfect actor for the role of Doctor Who. Because it's such a difficult role. To be able to navigate the nutty professor aspect of it, at times almost physical comedy, with the emotional intelligence and truth that is required, there are not many roles that throw those kind of challenges at you, and he was just fantastic. So with Matt, it was about guiding him to where I felt he needed to go, but more often than not his instinct took him there anyway. He's just brilliant, and a wonderful human being to work with, we got on brilliantly.

WS: That climactic speech is interesting, because obviously it's followed up with Clara coming in to save the day. How did the addition of Jenna into that scene affect its overall shape?

FB: I think the key to that is to get both actors talking about the scene and sharing thoughts and ideas. Even though they have two very distinct speeches, they have their own moments within that scene, in a way we treated the whole scene as one performance they were sharing. We had to discuss what the objective of the scene was, where we wanted to be at the end of the episode, and make sure the two characters combined to achieve it, and I think we did that pretty successfully. And of course, Jenna was a spectator throughout Matt's speech. I think she would freely admit that watching the level of emotion that he reached really helped her gauge where she needed to step in. So it was about making it one conversation between the three of us, rather than me talking separately to both of them.

WS: Where did you want the characters to be at the end of the episode?

FB: I can't remember one hundred per cent, but obviously you always look at the objective of the script. How do we need to end this, and what's the best way to defeat the foe at that point? In terms of Matt's performance, we agreed that he needed to feel completely spent emotionally, as a character, and he certainly was as an actor. Because it had to give Clara the motivation to come in and rescue the situation, seeing the Doctor giving his absolute all, and it just not being quite enough. She had to steel herself and find the courage to put herself in a situation that she has never been in before. It's a situation that she subsequently understands, this is the way it's going to be, this is what I'm entering into, if I'm going to travel round with this guy everyone calls the Doctor.

WS: Both Jenna and Matt have very intense one-on-one conversations with Emilia's character within the episode. How did you approach these two conversations?

FB: Those scenes are about Clara and the Doctor being the grown-up characters, imparting wisdom. We discussed the sensitive nature in which we wanted to deliver those lines. In terms of Emilia, I just asked her to really listen to them, you know, listen like it's the first time, even though it might have been five or six takes in, listen and respond as naturally as you can. I try not to be prescriptive, I like to make sure there is some room for manoeuvre, and not every single take has to be exactly the same. I discussed this with Jenna quite a bit: we wanted her to try and embody a kind of 'big sister' figure for Merry. Because that's essentially what Clara does, from the moment she follows Merry into the warehouse when she's being chased by the Vigil. It was very much a big sister rather than a maternal kind of relationship. There's that lovely moment behind the TARDIS where Clara recounts her fears, where she says, 'We're all afraid of something, and mine was getting lost when I was little.' You have to relate on that level, so I told Jenna, 'Try and take yourself back to your own childhood, and put yourself in Merry's shoes.'

With Matt it was just about making sure he made Merry feel safe. His job at that point was to protect her. But also because, being the Doctor, sometimes protecting someone is telling them a truth that might not be comfortable, it might not necessarily be wrapping someone up in cotton wool. It's about understanding a character is mature enough to tell them the truth. That's something we worked on as well, the dynamic between the Doctor and Merry. Because you know, what was happening to her was despicable, given that she's a child. I mean, she was being offered up as a sacrifice! So again, there were times when Matt and I talked about this, and I said, 'Try and empower her, make her feel that she's not this sort of weak, scared little child.' If I remember rightly, there was a story he told about her being unique in this universe, unique and original, and that was a sort of empowering speech. It was about making sure all those things landed, really.

WS: Were you conscious of walking a line, between that safety and comfort the Doctor and Clara present, and the really quite horrifying situation the character is in?

FB: Yes, I think so. Again it boils down to being as truthful as you can, in a constructed environment. It doesn't matter if you're a 10-year-old actor or a 50-year-old actor, no-one wants to put in a bad performance, and Emilia was the same. She was conscious that she had to be afraid of the creature in the glass, of Grandfather, but she didn't want to be seen as a screaming, wailing little kid. That would have been inappropriate for the story, because one of the important things about her character is that she is wise beyond her years. The reason she'd been chosen as a sacrifice was because she's full of stories, of age and experience, and there's a lot to her to consume. So she behaved appropriately for a character that young, but also got the nuances of why she'd been chosen, and gave her a sense of maturity that was believable in that scenario.

WS: What is your sense of Merry as a character, and her arc across the episode?

FB: Well, I think there's a reason why she was chosen, there's a maturity and an age beyond her years. But I think in many ways, her arc was kind of about reversing that. So rather than developing that sense of maturity, in a sense her arc was more about trying to relieve her of that, and allowing her to be a child again. It's almost like removing the ageing process, and allowing her, after the story's ended, to not have to shoulder that responsibility any more, allowing her to go back to being a child of 10 or 11 years old.

WS: To what extent were you involved in creating the episode's music? Was it all ready when you started filming?

FB: There wasn't really a lot, to begin with. I actually got quite panicky about it as we got closer and closer to production, because we didn't have a song [for the religious ceremony]. The song was referred to on the page as 'The Long Song,' but there was no song written, no lyrics in the script. Obviously as we got closer to production I made it very clear that we need this song written, we need it to go into the shoot, because actors are going to need to lip-sync to the song. Scenes are going to intercut, and they're going to weave in and out of one another, but the song is continually sung, so if we don't have the song available we are going to come up against all kinds of timing issues when we get into post-production. So that spurred everyone on, and I had discussions with Murray Gold about the nature of this song. He started to put some sketches together, we would listen to them and shape them accordingly, and swap a few ideas.

Eventually we had the song ready to go into the shoot with, so that we could use playback on set, and make sure that everyone was able to lip-sync. Because the actors, especially the Chorister in the Temple, he needed to get the timing of the song right in his head. When you're shooting, obviously he has to mime and you can't have any music playing, otherwise it would be all over the other dialogue. So we had to play that in and cut the music, and the Chorister had to be able to continue singing the lyrics of the song, in the correct timing, so that when we put the song back on afterwards in post-production, everything matched. So it was crucial to get that song ready and available to us for the shoot.

WS: You mention you were involved in helping put the song together. What were you after in the Long Song?

FB: In truth, what the Long Song is, is a lullaby. So we had to do our **Doctor Who** version of a lullaby, not all sort of warm and fluffy and cutesy, but something that has believably kept the Old God in slumber for time immemorial. But it also needed to have that slight undercurrent of darkness, that suggested something Other, and foreshadowed some of the danger there would be if the Old God woke. When the Chorister starts to get a sense that something is changing, there's a subtle shift in the tone of the Long Song, and it shifts into something slightly more dark and dangerous. So we discussed those sorts of pivotal shifts in the Long Song, which were crucial to get right as well.

WS: Looking back on *The Rings of Akhaten* now, is there anything you're particularly proud of?

FB: I'm very proud of it, as an episode. It's not without its shortcomings. One of the things I like the most is that it's proved very divisive between **Doctor Who** fans. I love doing things that spark debate, and contrasting opinions. I'd much rather that than people generally watching stuff and going, 'Yeah, that was OK.' I'm very pleased that I've read some reviews, a time after, saying 'Do you know what, I think people were unfair on *The Rings of Akhaten*, and when you look at it, it's incredibly layered and complex, and I think it's one of the best **Doctor Who** episodes there's been.' So that was great. I'm really proud of the visual side of things. It was incredibly challenging, because literally half an episode we were looking at greenscreen, so we had to make sure we conceived of all our visual ideas in a way that would be believable. I'm also very proud of the performances, because again, when you're shooting 20, 25 minutes of an episode against greenscreen, and still reaching those levels of emotional performance, that's something to be very proud of. And I really like the moment Clara steps out of the TARDIS, when she sees the planet for the first time. It still makes me smile, and gives me a kind of warm feeling. So yeah, there's a lot to be proud of, I think.

WS: As well you should be, though I'm obviously biased. To what extent were you paying attention to the episode's reception?

FB: To be honest, I'm not someone who really worries about reviews. I read some of them, but so long as I feel I've done everything I can, I'm not sure what's to be gained by worrying too much about what everyone else thinks. Of course you want people to like what you do, and going into production, you're acutely aware of the responsibility of being a director on **Doctor Who**. You know it has an incredibly passionate, an incredibly loyal, yet at times a really unforgiving, fanbase. And of course you want to keep everybody happy, but that's impossible. Going into it, I was certainly aware of the responsibility on my shoulders, in terms of delivering an episode that the **Doctor Who** fanbase would enjoy.

WS: One of the things I find most interesting about *The Rings of Akhaten* is that sense of childlike wonder. Was that something you were consciously aiming for?

FB: I think it was. We wanted to take people as far as we could, on a television show, and a television budget, back to their childhoods, how they felt watching **Star Wars**, how they felt watching **Indiana**

Jones, just being literally transported to an alien planet, was something that motivated all of us. We really want people to be beaming with smiles at what they're seeing. We want them to be able to feel the heat, and smell the smells of the market, and really put them in that place, and just take them on a real rollercoaster ride. So yes, awe and wonder were buzzwords for this episode, most definitely. They were go-to descriptions for what we wanted to achieve.

WS: Looking back on the episode now, is there anything that you'd do differently?

FB: One of the things I really liked, but think was under-used, was actually the Vigil. I think they had a lot of potential, to have a greater impact on the episode, and on Merry's journey as a character, and I think that was a little under-exploited. I slightly regret that, and I wonder, perhaps, if we had the time again, whether we could use the Vigil to greater effect. There are a couple of practical things I would have liked to have just got a little bit better. This is one thing that I know some people have picked up on: the speed bike sequence felt like it didn't quite measure up to the rest of the visual effects [VFX]. And also, perhaps, the VFX for the planet itself at the end. Looking back now, we wanted to try and humanise the planet, we didn't literally want to put a face on it. We wanted to create shadings that suggested there was some kind of face beneath that was reactive, but I think it perhaps ended up being a bit too much like just a face on the planet. So I might try and do that differently. But those things are incredibly hard to do, and that was very challenging at the time. How do you add a human element to that planet? It's kind of a ball of fire, really. There aren't many ways you can go about doing it. So it was incredibly challenging, but we might perhaps look at that slightly differently if we had the chance to do it again.

WS: Any final thoughts about *The Rings of Akhaten*?

FB: You know, just preparing to chat to you, I went back over a few of the reviews, and I do like the fact that lots of people are far kinder to it than I remember. I read something today, there was an article called '10 Reasons Why *The Rings of Akhaten* is the Best Episode Ever,' or something like that[266]. So I think we've been vindicated, or I hope we have.

---

266 Hurd, '10 Reasons *The Rings of Akhaten* Is the Best Episode Since *The Eleventh Hour*'.

APPENDIX 3: DIRECTOR'S STATEMENT BY FARREN BLACKBURN

This document was written early on in the production of The Rings of Akhaten *(hence the working title, 'Alien Planet'). It was intended to outline the director's vision for the story. It is reproduced here, in its original form, by kind permission of Farren Blackburn.*

ALIEN PLANET

DIRECTOR'S STATEMENT

Alien Planet is Indiana Jones in Space. And never let us forget the space bit. Classic high octane action adventure given a sci-fi tip at every turn. Raiders meets The Mummy versus Prometheus with a hint of Blade Runner for good measure.

The episode will bear all the hallmarks of what we've come to expect from Dr Who, navigating action, danger, horror, humour, pathos and emotion shot through with an epic cinematic style.

We have chances in abundance to lull the audience into a false sense of security, counter-pointing the gentle sacred lament of the choristers Long Song with Clara's domesticity before the Doctor plucks both her and the audience out for the ride of their lives to the spaciest planet we've seen, populated by the zaniest aliens and the scariest monsters.

And here the Doctor will relish showing Clara the infinite possibilities of time travel adventure, taking us with him through Clara's eyes as she goes on a journey that impacts personally and carries an emotional resonance for her.

We will bear witness to an epic onslaught on Clara's senses as she experiences the thrills and spills of an alien planet, a weird yet exciting universe and the sense of a civilization that pre-exists human history.

In this context, earth is nothing but a grain of sand on a vast and limitless beach but Clara will soon learn the difference one person can make.

And so we're thrust into Tiaanamaat, a vibrant melting pot of alien cultures cast in the light from the imposing planet Akhaten.

Though it's an alien world, there will be a sense of the familiar about everything albeit with a sci-fi twist, maybe it's Aztec, possibly Inca or Ancient Egyptian, who knows for sure. The world is historic but modern, basic but space age, a huge contradiction in so many terms but so vivid we will experience the energy, feel the heat and smell the smells.

Depicted in bold, brazen frames, graphic wides, hues of light and colour it will be a seductive yet strangely alien habitat. As we explore our way around it we will be with the Doctor and Clara, literally, every inch of the way. An energetic roving camera will soak up the sights and sounds around, tracking on their shoulders carrying us with them, tracking back in their faces showing us their excitement, awe, wonder, hopes and fears then thrusting us into their POV and with it their predicament and dilemma.

The Doctor will stride confidently through the episode, bang in the centre of frame, chasing into epic wide angle close ups, not just hero shots but superhero shots, all the time his infectious enthusiasm drawing Clara in its wake.

But this is Dr Who and so inevitably what starts out as a fun romp through the hustling and bustling streets of Tiaanamaat soon catapults our heroes into jeopardy as the rings align and the Old God of the Planet Akhaten threatens to wake.

With the fate of the innocent Merry and the whole alien population hanging in the balance it's now that Clara is set to truly learn what the Doctor means when he says, 'We don't walk away…..' It's now that she will start to fully understand, if she didn't already, quite what she's in for and how true companionship can only ever be built on trust, loyalty, respect, affection even!!!!

As the Old God shifts and stirs, so too will the tone of the episode with the visual palette moving from seductive colours to cooler shades, from warm light to shadowy dark, peppering the atmosphere with a growing sense of tension where even the Long Song, a beautiful lamenting lullaby at the start now seems strangely foreboding. But all the time the impending danger will still be undercut by the Doctor's wit and sense of fun.

Framings may slip slightly off kilter as the world around the Doctor poses its threat. The Doctor and Clara, once confidently united on screen may now find themselves more isolated in the frames as they each become separated and vulnerable.

As the Doctor and Clara are drawn ever deeper into the plight of Merry and the inhabitants of Akhaten, venturing into the unknown, the action adventure will go into overdrive in a race against time to save the day.

The episode will have a distinctly original rhythm, intercutting slower almost dreamlike sequences dictated by the pace of the Long Song with action sequences of gathering momentum that have the distinct sense of a ticking clock building to an almost orchestral crescendo of action and interplay before re-establishing the calm of the episode's original status quo.

Music in no small part will be vital. And Alien Planet will be pure cinema on the small screen.

I'm excited. Are you???

BIBLIOGRAPHY

Books

Adams, Douglas, *The Hitchhiker's Guide to the Galaxy*. 1979. London, Pan Books, 2009. ISBN 9780330508537.

Adams, Douglas, *The Restaurant at the End of the Universe*. London, Pan Books, 1980. ISBN 9780330262132.

Arnold, Jon, *The Eleventh Hour*. **The Black Archive** #19. Edinburgh, Obverse Books, 2018. ISBN 9781909031685.

Collins, Sophie, *Who Is Mary Sue?* London, Faber & Faber, 2018. ISBN 9780571346615.

Davies, Russell T, et al, *Doctor Who: The Shooting Scripts*. London, BBC Books, 2005. ISBN 9780563486411.

Dawkins, Richard, *The Selfish Gene*. 1976. Oxford, Oxford University Press, 2016. ISBN 9780198788607.

Dawkins, Richard, *The God Delusion*. 2006. London, Bantam Press, 2016. ISBN 9781784161927.

Dawkins, Richard, *Outgrowing God: A Beginner's Guide*. London, Bantam Press, 2019. ISBN 9781787631212.

Dennett, Daniel C, *Breaking the Spell: Religion As a Natural Phenomenon*. 2006. London, Penguin Books, 2007. ISBN 9780141017778.

Eagleton, Terry, *Reason, Faith, and Revolution: Reflections on the God Debate*. New Haven and London, Yale University Press, 2009. ISBN 9780300164534.

Franke, Alyssa, *Hell Bent*. **The Black Archive** #22. Edinburgh, Obverse Books, 2018. ISBN 9781909031715.

Gandhi, Leela, *Postcolonial Theory: A Critical Introduction*. Crows Nest, Allen & Unwin, 1998. ISBN 1864484314.

Hansen, Christopher J, ed, *Ruminations, Peregrinations and Regenerations: A Critical Approach to Doctor Who*. Newcastle upon Tyne, Cambridge Scholars Publishing, 2010. ISBN 9781443820844.

> Amy-Chinn, Dee, 'Davies, Dawkins, and Deus Ex TARDIS: Who Finds God in the Doctor?'

Harris, Sam, *The End of Faith: Religion, Terror, and the Future of Reason*. 2004. London, Simon & Schuster, 2006. ISBN 9780743268097.

Hills, Matt, ed, *New Dimensions of Doctor Who: Adventures in Space, Time and Television*. London and New York, IB Tauris, 2014. ISBN 9781845118662.

> Hills, Matt, 'Anniversary Adventures in Space and Time: The Changing Faces of **Doctor Who**'s Commemoration'.

Hills, Matt, *Doctor Who: The Unfolding Event – Marketing, Merchandising and Mediatizing a Brand Anniversary*, London, Palgrave Macmillan, 2015. ISBN 9781349558933.

Hind, Dan, *The Threat to Reason: How the Enlightenment was Hijacked and How We Can Reclaim It*. 2007. London, Verso, 2008. ISBN 9781844672530.

Hitchens, Christopher, *God is Not Great: How Religion Poisons Everything*. 2007. London, Atlantic Books, 2008. ISBN 9781843545743.

Hitchens, Christopher, Richard Dawkins, Sam Harris, and Daniel C Dennet, *The Four Horsemen: The Discussion That Sparked an Atheist Revolution*. London, Bantam Press, 2019. ISBN 9780593080399.

hooks, bell, *Feminist Theory: From Margin to Center*. Boston, South End Press, 1984. ISBN 9780896082212.

Kundnani, Arun, *The Muslims Are Coming!: Islamophobia, Extremism and the Domestic War on Terror*. 2014. London, Verso, 2015. ISBN 9781781685587.

Mill, John Stuart, *On Liberty, Utilitarianism, and Other Essays*. Oxford, Oxford University Press, 2015. ISBN 9780199670802.

Mohanty, Chandra Talpade, *Feminism Without Borders: Decolonizing Theory, Practicing Solidarity*. Durham and London, Duke University Press, 2003. ISBN 9780822330219.

Morgan, Robin, ed, *Sisterhood is Powerful: An Anthology of Writings from the Women's Liberation Movement*. New York, Vintage, 1970. ISBN 9780394705392.

   Morgan, Robin, 'Introduction: The Women's Revolution'.

Morgan, Robin, ed, *Sisterhood is Global: The International Women's Movement Anthology*. 1984. Middlesex, Penguin Books, 1985. ISBN 9781558611603.

   Morgan, Robin, 'Introduction: Planetary Feminism – The Politics of the 21st Century'.

O'Day, Andrew, ed, *Doctor Who: The Eleventh Hour – A Critical Celebration of the Matt Smith and Steven Moffat Era*. London and New York, IB Tauris, 2014. ISBN 9781780760193.

Amy-Chinn, Dee, 'Amy's Boys, River's Man: Generation, Gender and Sexuality in the Moffat Whoniverse'.

Cherry, Brigid, '"Oh, No, That Won't Do at All…It's ridiculous!": Observations on the **Doctor Who** Audience'.

Hewett, Richard, 'Who is Matt Smith? Performing the Doctor'.

Hexel, Vasco, 'Silence Won't Fall: Murray Gold's Music in the Steven Moffat Era'.

Kilburn, Matthew, 'Genealogies across Time: History and Storytelling in Steven Moffat's **Doctor Who**'.

Orman, Kate, *Pyramids of Mars*. **The Black Archive** #12. Edinburgh, Obverse Books, 2017. ISBN 9781909031579.

Orthia, Lindy, ed, *Doctor Who and Race*. Bristol, Intellect Books, 2013. ISBN 9781783200368.

Vohlidka, John, '**Doctor Who** and the Critique of Western Imperialism'.

Richardson, Louise, *What Terrorists Want: Understanding the Enemy, Containing the Threat*. 2006. New York, Random House, 2007. ISBN 9780812975444.

Said, Edward W, *Orientalism*. 1978. London, Penguin Books, 2003. ISBN 9780141187426.

Sastim, Defne, and Caitlin Smith, eds, *101 Claras to See*. 2016. No ISBN.

Burnard, Kevin, 'Egomaniac Needy Storytelller'.

Smith, Caitlin, 'Masked'.

Shaw, Ian, ed, *The Oxford History of Ancient Egypt*. 2000. Oxford and New York, Oxford University Press, 2003. ISBN 9780192804587.

Van Dijk, Jacobus, 'The Amarna Period and the Later New Kingdom (c 1352-1069 BC)'.

Shukla, Nikesh, ed, *The Good Immigrant*. London, Unbound, 2017. ISBN 9781783523955.

Chetty, Darren, '"You Can't Say That! Stories Have To Be About White People"'.

Smith, Barbara, ed, *Home Girls: A Black Feminist Anthology*. New York, Kitchen Table: Women of Color Press, 1983. ISBN 9780913175026.

Reagon, Bernice Johnson, 'Coalition Politics: Turning the Century'.

Young, Robert JC, *Postcolonialism: A Very Short Introduction*. Oxford, Oxford University Press, 2003. ISBN 9780192801821.

Periodicals

Doctor Who Magazine (DWM). Marvel UK, Panini, BBC, 1979-.

Arnopp, Jason, 'Oh, My Stars!' DWM #464, cover date October 2013.

Cook, Benjamin, 'The Rings of Akhaten'. DWM #459, cover date May 2013.

Griffiths, Peter, 'The Results In Full!' DWM #474, cover date July 2014.

Griffiths, Peter, 'The Data of the Doctor!' DWM #474, cover date July 2014.

Kibble-White, Graham, '*The Rings of Akhaten*'. DWM #460, cover date June 2013.

Kibble-White, Graham, '*Hide*'. DWM #460, cover date June 2013.

Moffat, Steven, 'Production Notes'. DWM #405, cover date March 2009.

Doctor Who: The Complete History Volume 73: *The Rings of Akhaten, Cold War, Hide* and *Journey to the Centre of the TARDIS*. Panini UK Ltd, 2016.

Lash, Nicholas, 'Where does *The God Delusion* come from?' *New Blackfriars*. Volume 80, Issue 1017, 2007, pp507-21.

Moore, Leah, John Reppion, and Ben Templesmith, *Doctor Who: The Whispering Gallery*. IDW Publishing, 2009.

Spivak, Gayatri Chakravorty, 'French Feminism in an International Frame'. *Yale French Studies*. No. 62, *Feminist Readings: French Texts/American Contexts*, 1981, pp154-84.

Television

Battlestar Galactica. Glen A Larson Productions, Universal Television, ABC, 1978-79.

Lost Planet of the Gods, 1978.

Doctor Who. BBC, 1963-.

The Complete Fifth Series. DVD release, 2010.

'Additional Scene'. DVD extra.

The Complete Seventh Series. DVD release, 2013.

'The Bells of Saint John: A Prequel'. DVD extra.

Doctor Who Confidential. BBC, 2005-11.

Do You Remember The First Time?, 2007.

Hard Sun. BBC, Hulu, Euston Films, Freemantle Media, 2018.

Luther. BBC, 2010-.

Series 1, Episode 1, 2010.

Series 1, Episode 2, 2010.

Series 2, Episode 2, 2011.

Series 3, Episode 3, 2013.

Series 3, Episode 4, 2013.

Series 5, Episode 2, 2019.

The Enemies of Reason. Channel 4, 2007.

The Irrational Health Service, 2007.

The Root of All Evil?. Channel 4, 2006.

Whistle and I'll Come to You. BBC, 2010.

Film

Braff, Zach, dir, *Garden State*, Camelot Pictures, Jersey Films, Double Features Films, Fox Searchlight Pictures, Miramax, 2004.

Crowe, Cameron, dir, *Elizabethtown*, Cruise/Wagner Productions, Vinyl Films, Paramount Pictures, 2005.

Edwards, Blake, dir, *Breakfast at Tiffany's*, Jurow-Shepherd, Paramount Pictures, 1961.

Lucas, George, dir, *Star Wars*, Lucasfilm, 20th Century Fox, 1977.

Newell, Mike, dir, *Four Weddings and a Funeral*, PolyGram Filmed Entertainment, Channel Four Films, Working Title Films, 1994.

Webb, Marc, dir, *500 Days of Summer*, Dune Entertainment, Fox Searchlight Pictures, 2009.

Audio CD

Gold, Murray, *Doctor Who: Series 7 – Original Television Soundtrack*. BBC Worldwide, 2013.

Robson, Eddie, *Phobos*. **Doctor Who: The Eighth Doctor Adventures**. Big Finish Productions, 2007.

Web

'**Doctor Who** 50th Is the Most Watched Drama in 2013'. BBC, 3 December 2013. https://www.bbc.co.uk/blogs/doctorwho/entries/ef1574ba-3a01-3d70-ad00-87782c08e2c2. Accessed 5 August 2019.

'Emmy Winners and Nominees 2011: Complete List'. The Hollywood Reporter, 18 September 2011. https://www.hollywoodreporter.com/news/emmy-nominations-2011-full-list-211331. Accessed 10 November 2019."

'Emmy Winners and Nominees 2012: The Complete List'. The Hollywood Reporter, 23 September 2012. https://www.hollywoodreporter.com/news/emmy-2012-winners-nominees-complete-list-373169. Accessed 10 November 2019.

'Epic Images for the New Adventures'. BBC, 2013. https://www.bbc.co.uk/programmes/p016fx8z/p016fx5x. Accessed

31 October 2019.

'Golden Globes 2012: The Winners List'. The Hollywood Reporter, 15 January 2012. https://www.hollywoodreporter.com/news/golden-globes-2012-winners-list-282032. Accessed 10 November 2019.

'Moffat on Diversity in **Doctor Who**: "We Must Do Better"'. Doctor Who TV, 30 May 2016. http://www.doctorwhotv.co.uk/moffat-on-diversity-in-doctor-who-we-must-do-better-80637.htm. Accessed 5 August 2019.

'Religious hate crimes: Rise in offences recorded by police'. BBC, 16 October 2018. https://www.bbc.co.uk/news/uk-45874265. Accessed 5 August 2019.

'Shabcast 23b: New Atheism is the Opium of Misogynists, Islamophobes, and Imperialists'. Libsyn, 11 August 2016. http://pexlives.libsyn.com/shabcast-23b-new-atheism-is-the-opium-of-misogynists-islamophobes-and-imperialists. Accessed 5 August 2019.

'What Millennials' YouTube Usage Tells Us about the Future of Video Viewership'. Comscore, 23 June 2016. https://www.comscore.com/Insights/Blog/What-Millennials-YouTube-Usage-Tells-Us-about-the-Future-of-Video-Viewership. Accessed 19 February 2020.

Anders, Charlie Jane, '**Doctor Who**'s Steven Moffat: The io9 Interview'. io9, 18 May 2010. https://io9.gizmodo.com/doctor-whos-steven-moffat-the-io9-interview-5542010. Accessed 5 August 2019.

Anders, Charlie Jane, '**Doctor Who**'s New Companion Is Only

Lovable When the Show Isn't Trying to Make Us Love Her'. io9, 7 April 2013. https://io9.gizmodo.com/doctor-whos-new-companion-is-only-lovable-when-the-sho-471022453. Accessed 5 August 2019.

Anders, Charlie Jane, 'Please Stop Spreading This Nonsense that Rey From **Star Wars** Is a "Mary Sue"'. io9, 21 December 2015. https://io9.gizmodo.com/please-stop-spreading-this-nonsense-that-rey-from-star-1749134275. Accessed 5 August 2019.

Anderson, Kyle, '**Doctor Who** Review: *The Rings of Akhaten*'. Nerdist, 6 April 2013. https://archive.nerdist.com/doctor-who-review-the-rings-of-akhaten/. Accessed 10 November 2019.

Anderson, Kyle, 'Steven Moffat On Clara Becoming the Doctor in **Doctor Who** Series 8'. Nerdist, 15 December 2014. https://archive.nerdist.com/steven-moffat-on-clara-becoming-the-doctor-in-series-8/. Accessed 5 August 2019.

Bartyzel, Monika, ''Girls on Film: Why It's Time to Retire the Term "Manic Pixie Dream Girl"'. The Week, 23 April 2013. https://theweek.com/articles/465113/girls-film-why-time-retire-term-manic-pixie-dream-girl. Accessed 5 August 2019.

BBC Studios, '"I. AM. TALKING!" – **Doctor Who** – BBC'. YouTube, 20 April 2011. https://www.youtube.com/watch?v=5ecycHAZtaM. Accessed 5 August 2019.

Bean, Brad, 'Paul McGann Reads Pandorica Speech at Cincinnati Comic Expo'. YouTube, 21 September 2014. https://www.youtube.com/watch?v=pBWgPIZlh94. Accessed 5 August 2019.

Brew, Simon, '**Doctor Who** Series 7: *The Rings of Akhaten* Review'. Den of Geek, 6 April 2013. https://www.denofgeek.com/tv/doctor-

who/25115/doctor-who-series-7-the-rings-of-akhaten-review.
Accessed 5 August 2019.

Campbell, Jane, 'The Arc of Alchemy (**Doctor Who**: Season 20)'.
Eruditorum Press, 2015.
http://www.eruditorumpress.com/blog/the-arc-of-alchemy-doctor-
who-season-twenty/. Accessed 5 August 2019.

Campbell, Jane, 'The Circle in the Square (**Doctor Who**)'.
Eruditorum Press, 2016.
http://www.eruditorumpress.com/blog/the-circle-in-the-square-
doctor-who/. Accessed 5 August 2019.

Clement, J, 'Percentage of US Internet Users Who Use YouTube As
Of 3rd Quarter 2019, By Age Group'. Statista, 10 October 2019.
https://www.statista.com/statistics/296227/us-youtube-reach-age-
gender/. Accessed 19 February 2020.

Connolly, Kelly, 'The Radical Helplessness of the New **Doctor Who**'.
The Atlantic, 10 December 2018.
https://www.theatlantic.com/entertainment/archive/2018/12/doct
or-who-radical-helplessness-jodie-whittaker-season-11/577741/.
Accessed 5 August 2019.

Crossley, Elliott, 'Impression #3.5 – 10th Doctor (*Rings of Akhaten*)'.
YouTube, 19 October 2014.
https://www.youtube.com/watch?v=gM6oIdP4QtM. Accessed 5
August 2019.

DantheGlassesMan, 'Matt Smith Impersonation – *Rings of Akhaten*
Speech'. YouTube, 14 June 2014.
https://www.youtube.com/watch?v=6TkK9mQNCgw. Accessed 5
August 2019.

Doctor Who YouTube Channel, 'Speech to Akhaten | *The Rings of Akhaten* | **Doctor Who**'. YouTube, 7 January 2014. https://www.youtube.com/watch?v=GoVLhUxhdSw. Accessed 5 August 2019.

Graham, Jack, 'Steven Moffat: A Case For The Prosecution'. Eruditorum Press, 2014. http://www.eruditorumpress.com/blog/guest-post-steven-moffat-a-case-for-the-prosecution/. Accessed 5 August 2019.

Graham, Jack, 'Empires and Metaphors'. Eruditorum Press, 2018. http://www.eruditorumpress.com/blog/empires-and-metaphors/. Accessed 5 August 2019.

Hadoke, Toby, 'Russell T Davies: Part 5'. **Toby Hadoke's Who's Round** #124. Big Finish Productions, June 2015. https://www.bigfinish.com/releases/v/toby-hadoke-s-who-s-round-124---russell-t-davies-part-5-1332. Accessed 5 August 2019.

Hadoke, Toby, 'Michael Pickwoad'. **Toby Hadoke's Who's Round** #138. Big Finish Productions, September 2015. https://www.bigfinish.com/releases/v/toby-hadoke-s-who-s-round-138-michael-pickwoad-1397. Accessed 5 August 2019.

Haidrani, Salma, '"Islamophobic bullying made school a nightmare"'. BBC Three, 18 April 2019. https://www.bbc.co.uk/bbcthree/article/be8f4f0b-02aa-43d3-9924-f22c23263ecb. Accessed 5 August 2019.

Hamburger, Jacob, 'What Was New Atheism?'. The Point, 2019. https://thepointmag.com/2019/politics/what-was-new-atheism. Accessed 5 August 2019.

hbk51385, 'Colin Baker Reads the Pandorica Speech (**Doctor Who**)'.

YouTube, 8 February 2015.
https://www.youtube.com/watch?v=pu8eMIHfPkY. Accessed 5
August 2019.

Hitchens, Christopher, 'Londonistan Calling'. *Vanity Fair*, 2 May
2007. https://www.vanityfair.com/news/2007/06/hitchens200706.
Accessed 5 August 2019.

Hitchens, Christopher, 'Defending Islamofascism'. *Slate*, 22 October
2007. https://slate.com/news-and-politics/2007/10/defending-the-
term-islamofascism.html. Accessed 5 August 2019.

Hurd, Matthew, '**Doctor Who**: 10 Reasons *The Rings of Akhaten* Is
The Best Episode Since *The Eleventh Hour*'. WhatCulture, 11 April
2013. http://whatculture.com/tv/doctor-who-10-reasons-the-rings-
of-akhaten-is-the-best-episode-since-the-11th-hour?. Accessed 5
August 2019.

Jeffrey, Morgan, '"**Doctor Who**": New Episode "*The Rings of
Akhaten*" Review'. Digital Spy, 6 April 2013.
https://www.digitalspy.com/tv/cult/a470250/doctor-who-new-
episode-the-rings-of-akhaten-review/. Accessed 5 August 2019.

Kahn, Chuck, '*The Rings of Akhaten* Read by Colin Baker (Sixth
Doctor)'. YouTube, 25 August 2013.
https://www.youtube.com/watch?v=FiM4AfGwnZs. Accessed 5
August 2019.

Kilburn, Matthew, '**Doctor Who** XXXVII/11.6: *Demons of the
Punjab*'. The Event Library, 17 November 2018.
https://theeventlibrary.wordpress.com/2018/11/17/doctor-who-
xxxvii-11-6-demons-of-the-punjab/. Accessed 5 August 2019.

Martin, Dan, '**Doctor Who**: *The Rings of Akhaten* – Series 33,

Episode seven'. The Guardian, 6 April 2013. https://www.theguardian.com/tv-and-radio/tvandradioblog/2013/apr/06/doctor-who-rings-of-akhaten. Accessed 5 August 2019.

McAlpine, Fraser, 'The Secret of Matt Smith's Success as the 11th Doctor'. BBC America, 2013. http://www.bbcamerica.com/anglophenia/2013/12/secret-matt-smiths-success-eleventh-doctor. Accessed 5 August 2019.

Myers, PZ, 'The Train Wreck That Was the New Atheism'. Free Thought Blogs, 25 January 2019. https://freethoughtblogs.com/pharyngula/2019/01/25/the-train-wreck-that-was-the-new-atheism/. Accessed 5 August 2019.

Oppenheimer, Mark, 'Will Misogyny Bring Down The Atheist Movement?' Buzzfeed, 12 September 2014. https://www.buzzfeed.com/markoppenheimer/will-misogyny-bring-down-the-atheist-movement?. Accessed 5 August 2019.

Phillips, Tom, 'Matt Smith: The Rise and Fall of the Hipster Doctor'. *The New Statesman*, 3 June 2013. https://www.newstatesman.com/culture/2013/06/matt-smith-rise-and-fall-hipster-doctor. Accessed 5 August 2019.

Poole, Steven, '*The Four Horsemen* Review – Whatever Happened to "New Atheism"?'. *The Guardian*, 31 January 2019. https://www.theguardian.com/books/2019/jan/31/four-horsemen-review-what-happened-to-new-atheism-dawkins-hitchens. Accessed 5 August 2019.

Rabin, Nathan, 'The Bataan Death March of Whimsy Case File #1: *Elizabethtown*'. The AV Club, 25 January 2007.

https://film.avclub.com/the-bataan-death-march-of-whimsy-case-file-1-elizabet-1798210595. Accessed 5 August 2019.

Rabin, Nathan, 'I'm Sorry for Coining the Phrase "Manic Pixie Dream Girl"'. Salon, 16 July 2014. https://www.salon.com/control/2014/07/15/im_sorry_for_coining_the_phrase_manic_pixie_dream_girl/. Accessed 5 August 2019.

Richard Dawkins Foundation for Reason & Science, 'The Four Horsemen HD: Hour 1 of 2 – Discussions with Richard Dawkins, Ep 1'. YouTube, 22 February 2009. https://www.youtube.com/watch?v=9DKhc1pcDFM. Accessed 31 October 2019.

Richard Dawkins Foundation for Reason & Science, 'The Four Horsemen: Hour 2 of 2 – Discussions with Richard Dawkins, Ep 1'. YouTube, 24 February 2009. https://www.youtube.com/watch?v=TaeJf-Yia3A&t=2s. Accessed 31 October 2019.

Ruediger, Russ, '**Doctor Who** Recap: The Lord and the Rings'. *Vulture*, 7 April 2013. https://www.vulture.com/2013/04/doctor-who-recap-season-7-episode-8.html. Accessed 10 November 2019.

Sandifer, Elizabeth, 'My Mind Will Be Like That of a Child (*The Bells of Saint John*)'. Eruditorum Press, 2014. http://www.eruditorumpress.com/blog/my-mind-will-be-like-that-of-a-child-the-bells-of-saint-john/. Accessed 5 August 2019.

Sandifer, Elizabeth, 'Impossible Girl (*Hell Bent*)'. Eruditorum Press, 2018. http://www.eruditorumpress.com/blog/impossible-girl-hell-bent/. Accessed 5 August 2019.

Sandifer, Elizabeth, '*The Witchfinders* Review'. Eruditorum Press,

2018. http://www.eruditorumpress.com/blog/the-witchfinders-review/. Accessed 5 August 2019.

Sarkeesian, Anita, 'Tropes Vs Women #1: The Manic Pixie Dream Girl'. Feminist Frequency, 24 March 2011. https://feministfrequency.com/video/tropes-vs-women-1-the-manic-pixie-dream-girl/. Accessed 5 August 2019.

Smith, Caitlin, 'The Impossible Girl'. Eruditorum Press, 2014. http://www.eruditorumpress.com/blog/guest-post-the-impossible-girl/. Accessed 5 August 2019.

Snow, Mark, '**Doctor Who**: *"The Rings of Akhaten"* Review'. IGN, 6 April 2013. https://uk.ign.com/articles/2013/04/07/doctor-who-the-rings-of-akhaten-review. Accessed 5 August 2019.

Spencer, Caleb, 'Islamophobia: The Muslim Family Who "Ran Away" After Abuse'. BBC, 10 February 2019. https://www.bbc.co.uk/news/uk-wales-46990722. Accessed 5 August 2019.

Sproull, Patrick, 'Frank Cottrell-Boyce: "There are a lot of similarities between *Chitty Chitty Bang Bang* and **Doctor Who**"'. *The Guardian*, 18 August 2014. https://www.theguardian.com/childrens-books-site/2014/aug/18/frank-cottrell-boyce-chitty-bang-doctor-who. Accessed 5 August 2019.

Stylin' Steve, 'Peter Davison Reading Matt Smith's Pandorica Speech'. YouTube, 10 November 2013. https://www.youtube.com/watch?v=ezwG-h5l-48. Accessed 5 August 2019.

Sullivan, Shannon Patrick, '*The Daleks*'. *Doctor Who: A Brief History of Time (Travel)*. Shannon Patrick Sullivan, 24 March 2013.

http://www.shannonsullivan.com/doctorwho/serials/b.html.
Accessed 5 August 2019.

TARDISkey, '**Doctor Who** – Seventh Doctor – Pandorica Speech'.
YouTube, 11 September, 2011.
https://www.youtube.com/watch?v=nG9Z5djon7w. Accessed 5
August 2019.

TheSolarminiteBomb, 'Paul McGann Reads from *The Rings Of
Akhaten*'. YouTube, 27 September 2014.
https://www.youtube.com/watch?v=A64cZuIo_WM. Accessed 5
August 2019.

Torres, Phil, 'From the Enlightenment to the Dark Ages: How "New
Atheism" Slid Into the Alt-Right'. *Salon*, 29 July 2017.
https://www.salon.com/2017/07/29/from-the-enlightenment-to-
the-dark-ages-how-new-atheism-slid-into-the-alt-right/. Accessed 5
August 2019.

Walsh, Pete, 'Ninth Doctor – *Rings of Akhaten* Speech'. YouTube, 4
October 2017. https://www.youtube.com/watch?v=p6IhLSwbMwE.
Accessed 5 August 2019.

Weiss, Bari, 'Meet the Renegades of the Intellectual Dark Web'.
New York Times, 8 May 2018.
https://www.nytimes.com/2018/05/08/opinion/intellectual-dark-
web.html. Accessed 5 August 2019.

Wilkins, Alasdair, '**Doctor Who**: *The Rings of Akhaten*'. The AV Club,
6 April 2013. https://tv.avclub.com/doctor-who-the-rings-of-
akhaten-1798176389. Accessed 5 August 2019.

Wolf, Gary, 'The Church of the Non-Believers'. *Wired*, 1 November
2006. https://www.wired.com/2006/11/atheism/.

ACKNOWLEDGEMENTS

This book would not have been possible without a great deal of help from friends, family, editors, and colleagues.

Thank you to Jon Arnold, Jonne Bartelds, Ian Bayley, Melissa Beattie, James Blanchard, Ryan Bradley, Max Curtis, Judith Edmondson, Samantha Harden, Niki Haringsma, Georgia Harper, Alex Haruspis, Emma Jones, Christine Kelley, Matthew Kilburn, Adam Kranz, Ruth Long, Sam Maleski, Hetty Mosforth, Artur Nowrot, Paul Ritchie, John Salway, Sam Sheppard, Caitlin Smith, and Max Tuthill for your insightful comments on earlier versions of this manuscript. Your feedback has been vital in shaping this project.

Thank you to Tomer Feiner, Jack Graham, Nate Lynch, Molly Marsh, and Redha Rubaie for your help with research, and for your patient and well-informed tips on specialist subjects.

Thank you to the Oxford Doctor Who Society and the Facebook group Time And Relative Dimensions In Shitposting, who heard the lecture which eventually became this Black Archive.

Thank you to my editor, Philip Purser-Hallard, as well as Paul Simpson and Stuart Douglas. This book wouldn't have been half as good without you.

Thank you to Farren Blackburn for granting me an interview and permission to print your Director's Statement, and for being so patient and generous with your time.

And thank you to Lubabah Chowdhury, for your unwavering support throughout this process, and for sharing *The Rings of Akhaten* with me.

BIOGRAPHY

William Shaw is a writer, blogger, and poet from Sheffield, currently living in London. He has been watching **Doctor Who** since 2005, and writing for as long as he can remember. In 2015 he joined the Oxford Doctor Who Society, and was introduced to **Doctor Who** fandom at large. It is still one of the most welcoming and encouraging communities he has ever belonged to.

His non-fiction has appeared in *Doctor Who Magazine*, *Downtime*, *The Tides of Time*, and *The Oxford Culture Review*. His poetry has appeared in *Star*Line*, *The Martian Wave*, *Spaceports and Spidersilk*, *Scifaikuest*, *Nightsong*, and *Space and Time* magazine.

You can find him online at williamshawwriter.wordpress.com, or on Twitter @Will_S_7.